The Successful Single Mom

The Successful Single Mom

Published by Honorée Enterprises Publishing, LLC
Copyright 2009-2014 Honorée Enterprises Publishing, LLC

Printed in the United States of America.

ISBN 978-0-9980731-2-5

Check out all the titles in The Successful Single Mom book series:

Coming soon:

Dedication

Dedicated to you – the single mom. I wrote this book for you. You are in a class by yourself, and to be commended for your bravery, struggle and continued journey to success, joy and happiness. Here's to you, your children and the immeasurable difference you make in the world.

The Successful Single Mom Principles

1.   Discover the Real Truth

2.   Envision Your Exciting Future

3.   Assemble a Support Team & Ask for Help

4.   Expect and Create Magic and Miracles

5.   Prioritize Your Priorities

6.   Say Hello to Inner Peace

7.   Make a Plan & Set Goals for Your Amazing Future

8.   Give Back

Dear Reader,

Whether you are a single mom by chance or by choice, the tools, strategies and secrets to creating the inner peace, self-confidence and success you have been searching for are right here in this book. You are now well on your way to achieving the momentum and magical personal and professional success and happiness you've been dreaming about!

Its important to say this, right now at the very beginning: you don't *become* a "successful single mom," you already are one! Having said that, you may have some things you want to accomplish, another level you want to attain. What I really want for you is to be right here, right now, enjoying the journey while you feel how alive you are as you go for what you want.

I know you are here because you have wondered what would have to happen in order to "get your groove back" ... to feel healthy, centered and even optimistic again. During and after my divorce, I asked myself the questions you may have asked yourself: How do I raise a healthy, happy, well-adjusted child? How do I run a business, eliminate financial stress and feel like I am fulfilling my purpose for being on this planet? How do I heal and open myself up to a new love?

You have perhaps been struggling with the basic challenges every single mom faces, feeling helpless, overwhelmed or even depressed, having a lack of support, getting it all done, paying the bills and getting some sleep, balancing your personal and professional life. There are, of course, many others.

Six years ago I was a newly-divorced mom of a two-year old. I moved to a new city where I knew no-one and had no family. Present day, I am the proud mom of a 9-year old third-grader. We live in the home I bought just over a year ago and I run four successful companies. This book includes the processes and action steps I used after my separation and divorce to get and keep myself on track. Truthfully, most of the time I had to dig deep – I really wanted to stay in bed or on the couch (preferably with a gallon of Rocky Road). As a coach, however, I knew that I needed to use the tools I had in my tool box to create the life I wanted to live. I had to do it consistently and with intention.

In this book are the stories of women, just like you, who have walked the same path. I interviewed successful single moms, successful, by anyone's standards, to find out how they made it through. Some of their stories, thoughts, and ideas are included here to give you hope that one day soon all will be well. In addition, I selected a group of women – 7 in all – who completed the 100-day Transformation Program as a group. You'll meet Alisa, Christine, Julie, Kelly, Laurie, Vicky, and Melinda. Parts of their stories are here, too.

The best way to begin is to read through this entire book. Then, go back to the beginning and do all of the exercises to set yourself up for success. Be sure to follow the 100-Day Transformation Program as I've outlined it. Creating a new future can be daunting and overwhelming. By focusing on just the next 100 days – and taking them one day at a time – you will get where you want to go – or at the very least, you'll begin to make progress toward your goals. Perhaps you'll utilize personal coaching or create your own Successful Single Mom's Group as a base for support, information and advice. Remember: your new life is about you and what you want – for yourself and your children.

Note: You *can* have, do, be, create and enjoy whatever your heart desires. So go for it, 100%, for your 100 Days. As you share them with me and your fellow single moms, we'll celebrate your results all along the way, on the 100th Day and beyond!

This book is for every single mom, their friends and family... and for any mom considering going out on her own.

I've done it and you can, too! From my heart to yours, here's to your greatest success yet!

Honorée

Meet the Moms

For 100 days, I had the pleasure of working with these lovely women, who allowed me to coach, push, encourage and embrace them. They contributed their thoughts, ideas and best practices to the making of this book.

Alisa – mom to Sierra, age 8, and Tristan, age 3. Alisa is the founder of The Las Vegas Bellydance Intensive and Festival. She also owns AM Solutions, a web design company. She knew she needed a support network – joining the group reinforced her belief that when someone has support, they can create bigger and better things. She wants for you, dear reader, to create deep and intimate connections at all levels, including personally and spiritually.

Christine – mom to Jack, age 13, and Roger, age 15. Christine owns her newly established business, Mercury Permit Services in Las Vegas. Christine is now the ultimate optimist and hopes the single moms reading this book will find the courage to step out on their own, as she did, and know that they can do whatever they set their minds to.

Julie – mom to Hannah, age 4. Julie runs her own CPA firm, which she established during the course of the 100 days. "I hope this book helps the single moms reading it find the strength within to reclaim their power. Each mom can put her mind to something, follow her plan and with support will accomplish it."

Kelly – mom to 6 year old twins Sebastian and Miranda. Before her divorce, Kelly worked as the executive assistant at her former husband's family business for sixteen years. After a six month stay in Las Vegas with her sister, she now lives and works in California. She felt the program allowed her to find a rewarding job, and have people around her who cared about her for the first time – and wishes the same for you.

Laurie – mom to 5 year old Kevin. Laurie started her own business just prior to the start of our 100 day Program. She noticed that once she stopped focusing on the past, her attitude skyrocketed and her external results were blissful and powerful. Laurie wants you to know that no matter where your circumstances are, you can choose to find joy and be happy in every moment.

Vicky – mom to Michael, age 5. Michael has learning disabilities and Vicky is a high-powered executive and wants the readers to know that no matter how public your position, no matter how high up the ladder you've gotten, you must let your guard down with a carefully chosen group of people who will unconditionally support you. The rewards are amazing.

Melinda – mom to 10-year-old Angelica and 3-year-old Carson. She's a professional stock trader, inventor and budding entrepreneur. She loves to be of service to others, especially children – and operates from the philosophy of giving back. She feels like she's been blessed and has the need to share. She hopes the moms reading this book begin to believe in themselves. It may appear that every mom is successful, but the truth is we were all struggling and wanting more and that's why we came to do this Program.

TABLE OF CONTENTS

PROLOGUE

So THAT'S Why There are Two Parents!

Very early in my single mom adventure, and after another Saturday afternoon at the park, I ambitiously made lasagna for dinner, brownies for dessert and fresh pink lemonade. My daughter and I enjoyed a lovely dinner together and then got ready for one of our favorite activities: cuddle time. My three-year-old daughter Lexi curled up in my lap on the couch and fell asleep. A couple of hours later I carried her up to her room and put her to bed. It was late – around 11 p.m. – and I was delighted to not have an alarm to wake up to as it had been another long week in Single Mother Land. I had just fallen asleep when I heard Lexi crying and pulling herself up onto my bed. She said, "Mommy, I don't feel good!" and then proceeded to throw up her lasagna … and brownies … and pink lemonade … all over my big bed, its lovely white bedding and pretty decorative pillows. Oh my.

As my mom used to say, "What's a mother to do?"

She's scared, so I need to settle her down. Do I clean her up first or wash the linens? I can't leave her alone in the tub … Oh bloody hell.

The question I asked of myself was: how did I get here? I carried her into the tub, washed her off and put all of the linens and her pajamas in a big pile. Then we went and slept in the guest room. I wished in that moment I had an extra set of hands to help.

Further reflection made me realize that even when I had been married, those extra hands didn't exactly help. But I digress.

This was one of many nights I would think myself to sleep as I grappled with the situation, wondering how I could make it all work.

Here's the truth: In many ways, being a single mom can suck. Its hard. Its lonely. The days can seem endless and the nights are sometimes so quiet its deafening. Other times, it can be the best thing in the world! Now the schedule you set revolves completely around you and your children. You don't have to accommodate the needs, wants and desires of another adult and you can focus all of your free time on your children, yourself and your work. It can definitely be a roller coaster of thoughts, feelings and emotions. I wrote this book because when I was going through the process of finding myself and making my way, I needed some good news, a road map and some positive energy – basically a short list of things I could do to accelerate the process of feeling better and getting better results.

As a personal and business coach, I had all the tools at my disposal and yet it still took me quite a bit of time to catch my breath, get my bearings and start to create a plan. It was up to me to design my future and it took me awhile to realize that, and even longer to actually do it.

In a nutshell, here it is: sometimes its not so great and sometimes its fabulous. It will get better if it sucks, and it will better even if its fabulous. At the very least, it will start to suck less. You will begin to smile, and then laugh, and there will actually be some FUN. You may have become a single mom through the death of your spouse, or you may have chosen to be a single mom by adopting a child or simply choosing to separate from the father of your children. Regardless of how you got to be a single mom, you may be feeling some of the more challenging feelings I've been talking about here.

I began looking for the resource guide for "getting through the tunnel." The "tunnel" - that's what I call that period of my life – when I wasn't sure I was going to make it and I really wanted to. I didn't have much if any support – and I wanted that, too. I couldn't find *that* book, no matter where I searched. I had to find the tools on my own, experiment with them, put them into practice and find my way.

This book is *that* book. My wish for you is that you enjoy it, use it and love it – and that it rocks your world and changes your life for the better.

CHAPTER ONE

"OH SHIT" DAY

The Day that Turned Your Lives Upside Down

This day could have been yesterday, or perhaps it was ten years ago. The day you became a single mom is, without question, one of the hardest days of your life. This is the day many women have hoped for, regardless whether they come from an abusive, hopeless or simply dissatisfying situation, and yet dread at the same time. There's a chance you will have freedom: the opportunity to turn your life around and make it the way you want it ... then there's the reality check: how is it possible to get everything done and retain your sanity? Pay the bills? Raise the children?

My daughter went from being a happy, normal two-year-old one day, to being a clingy, needy, demanding, temper-tantrum throwing Tasmanian devil the next. She seemed to sense how unsettled I was feeling and almost instantly began reacting and acting out based upon my mental state. On top of my pending divorce, I now had a sick feeling in the pit of my stomach regarding how my daughter was going to be affected – short and long-term – by this new situation and the dark clouds over head. Here's the kicker: I didn't want to burden anyone with my feelings and insecurities, so sadly I kept most of them to myself. I didn't ask for help, I didn't know how. I didn't know what was going to happen next and I wasn't sure how to navigate what was coming.

Did you live that day in your mind a thousand times prior to it actually happening? Before I separated from my ex-husband, I used to think a lot (daydream is probably a better word) about what it would be like to be single again, have my freedom and raise my daughter on my own.

Then I would start to really think it through, and my mind filled with fear and uncertainty. I questioned and doubted. I came close to pushing the eject button for about two years before my actual Oh Shit! Day.

Can I tell you a secret? I was scared to death! I'm in a service business *and* self-employed, so I didn't have a regular paycheck. Would my income continue and could we not only survive but thrive if I went out on my own? I was living in Hawaii because my ex was stationed there in the military. Where should I move to? How would I get there? What would I do in terms of support when I got there? Doubt and trepidation kept me stuck for a really long time. If this resonates with you, trust me when I say you are truly not alone.

Although everything has ended up better than great, there were many times I wasn't sure the garden was growing roses!

Like I did, you may feel there is a seemingly endless list of things to do: dishes, laundry, shopping and other chores, in addition to work ... oh yes, and there's also providing emotional support to your child or children. I remember feeling overwhelmed at the daunting situation. Here's what I have discovered: its never all done, there are always at least two dozen things on my list ... laundry, organize the linen closet, hug my girl, buy school supplies, read email, return phone calls, get dog food, make food shopping list, drop off dry-cleaning, wash the car, finish manuscript ... more laundry ... sleep ...

What has worked for me is the act of surrender. I surrendered to the situation as it was as I was working toward how I wanted it to be. I also began to open my mind to the possibilities. I began to expect the best, and not be surprised when I got it. Once I cut myself some slack, upgraded my attitude to official positive status and raised my expectations, I was able to start to enjoy the days, relax into the time I spent with my daughter and actually make great progress toward my goals.

Take a Moment to Acknowledge Yourself

You are to be commended for your courage! Whether you chose to be a single mom or being a single mom was chosen for you, it takes a tremendous amount of guts to put one foot in front of the other, all on your own. Be sure to acknowledge yourself for using these circumstances as an opportunity to choose you, your future and the future of your children. Congratulations on reaching this new phase of your life - the best is yet to come.

Something Better is Coming

In the last six years, I've spoken to countless single moms. When asked the question: "What would you say to a new single mom?" the answer time and time again was a resounding, "There's a light at the end of the tunnel. Hang in there! It will get better. Someday you'll look back and realize every challenge has resulted in a blessing."

Sadly, no-one said that to me until I was already feeling better. I needed to hear it before that moment, and I hope you're hearing it just when you need it the most. I now say, "The light at the end of the tunnel is not an oncoming train!"

The *Successful Single Mom* is a woman who follows a set of principles, both to get her groove back and then to keep it. Success is how she defines it, whatever success means to her. You're a success just for picking up this book and being in the pursuit of your version of success. We'll explore these principles throughout the book, including the step-by-step instructions to get them implemented in your life. Here are those principles:

The Successful Single Mom Principles

1. Discover the Real Truth

2. Envision Your Exciting Future

3. Assemble a Support Team & Ask for Help

4. Expect and Create Magic and Miracles

5. Prioritize Your Priorities

6. Say Hello to Inner Peace

7. Make a Plan & Set Goals for Your Amazing Future

8. Give Back

Discover the Real Truth

Your self-esteem is most likely, in large part anyway, based upon what you've been told about yourself. We're all affected by what people say about us, even if we've chanted a million times, "Sticks and stones may break my bones, but words will never hurt me." Its time to excavate what's really true about you, and use that truth to move you forward.

Envision Your Exciting Future

When you were eight years old, if you wanted a bicycle, you wanted to get a new one all tricked out and one for each of your best friends. It was so easy to use your imagination first before you bugged your parents (constantly) to get you what you wanted, until you got it! Now is the time to awaken those "imagination juices," and get them flowing in order to become fully connected with the exciting life you're going to bring into being. In order to be able to attract those new and exciting results, you must begin to radiate more positive energy in order to attract more positive outcomes. The higher your personal vibration, the more opportunities that are going to come your way.

Said another way, you've got to have "good vibes" that open you to new, good stuff.

When I had a network marketing business years ago, my upline used to say, "Honorée, you've got to get excited and set yourself on fire! When you do, people will come from miles around to watch you burn!" Are you drawn to people who are passionate, excited, and on a mission? Of course you are! I know I am. I want to talk to them, get to know them, pick their brains, be around them, and help them achieve their goals. You've chosen you, now continue to do so by making your vision so real you can see it, taste it, feel it and believe it is on its way to you (right now!).

Assemble a Support Team & Ask for Help

Your Support Team consists of the people you can count on – really count on – no matter how low you get or how high you fly. They are your cheerleaders, they champion your causes, encouraging, pushing, hugging and tugging you to a better place and eventually your definition of success.

It is important to have this team in place and the sooner the better. Have someone to tell you how fantastic you are, on speed dial, ready for your call anytime 24/7. Just knowing they are there will make all the difference.

I am positive you need to be a strong member of your own support team. You will be alone sometimes and it will be easy in those moments to say things to yourself that are simply not helpful. You can rely on others, and you must also rely on yourself. We'll talk a lot about how to do that most effectively.

There are probably many people in your life that want to help yet are not quite sure what to do. Perhaps you want two hours to take a nap, or you simply need to do a bit more work to make ends meet. By all means reach out to other moms and offer to trade play dates. I did exactly that when I moved to Nevada from Hawaii five years ago. I didn't have a team of babysitters or know where to find any, and my closest family members were two thousand miles away. I had to get creative in order to attend the networking meetings that would allow me to grow my business, get my haircut or take a hot bath.

Here's some great news: people want to help you! You may find that some will offer to help, others won't. I know from personal experience that there are a number of people just waiting to feel useful, helpful and like they are making a difference. Now is your opportunity to allow them to give you that gift, a gift which you can pay forward a little later on.

Find a way to step through the fear, if that's what is holding you back. If its too hard to call, send an email. Alisa resonates with the fear. As a single mom, she knows how much is on her plate and its terribly difficult to want to burden another mom with more to do. Every mom feels like there's an endless list of things to do, whether she's single or not. Suck it up and ask anyway.

Expect and Create Magic and Miracles

Almost twenty years ago, I discovered the works of Eric Butterworth and Catherine Ponder, both teachers of spiritual laws. I learned from them – and the other works their work led me to – that while we live and operate by the natural laws on the physical plane, the truly powerful laws are mental and spiritual. An example of a physical law is the law of gravity. This law is in effect whether we know about it or not. Remember when you were watching your children learn how to walk? Karma is a well-known spiritual principle – what comes around goes around. Once you know it, you can use it for the greater good. Knowing the laws and how to navigate and use them will help you to effortlessly create bigger and better results quickly. When we tap into the laws, we are tapping into laws that are so powerful they can be used to multiply, neutralize or even reverse natural law. When we use them, they create results that seem truly magical and miraculous. In this book, I'm going to whet your appetite for this kind of information.

Prioritize Your Priorities

Many single moms fall into the superwoman trap, feeling that in addition to working all day, they must also keep a perfectly clean house, serve home-cooked meals, and tend to their children's every need. We have to be realistic about what we will and won't be able to accomplish in a day. In addition, we don't need to feel as though we have to overcompensate just because we are parenting on our own or going through a separation or divorce.

It is important to lower your expectations just a bit (or a lot!) and give yourself a break. It is certainly fine to serve cold cereal for breakfast or a fast-food meal for dinner every now and then, as long as your child's overall diet is healthy. There's no need to have a spotless house, what's important is the quality time you get to spend with your kids. Given the choice, I would much rather read The Magic Umbrella for the zillionth time than vacuum or dust (ok, the real truth is I would rather do almost anything than vacuum or dust, but you get the picture). Did your fondest childhood memories consist of living in an immaculate home or spending one-on-one time when your parents, where they focused just on you? If they didn't spend quality time with you, wouldn't it have felt better if they did?

In case it didn't occur to you, you are meant to be very high up on your priority list. As I write this, I'm flying from Las Vegas to Dallas, and for the umpteenth time I heard, "In case the cabin loses pressure, put the mask on yourself before you put it on any other adults or small children." That applies to your life right now – you must give to yourself what you need in order for you to be an effective anything – mom, friend, daughter, or employee.

Say Hello to Inner Peace

It is easy to feel massive amounts of guilt for the choices we have made, or may have been made for us. Whether we are single parents by chance or by choice, its natural to feel there's a lot wrong or lacking.

It's a great idea to focus on what is wonderful and amazing about your family then to dwell on what's missing or lacking. Many years ago, Oprah Winfrey suggested creating a gratitude journal. The exercise of writing down five things a day we're grateful for keeps your conscious and subconscious mind focused in the right direction, the direction you want to go in. By staying focused on where you want to go, you'll get there sooner. I have also found that by focusing on where I want to go, I'm able to let the daily bumps and challenges more easily roll off my back. I'm focused on what I want, and I don't expect the journey to be perfect – so when there are challenges it is easier to "be the ant that moves the plant."

Worrying is a lot of wasted energy that produces no solid, positive result. I know it is easy to do and to do often. You are better off utilizing the tools that are effective at bringing to fruition your goals and dreams. There are some "distracter activities" that are very effective and can keep your vibration high and the magical results consistently on their way to you. I'll share them with you in an upcoming chapter.

Make a Plan & Set Goals for Your Amazing Future

You are probably finding it hard to get through all the things on your to-do list each day. It is important to set daily, weekly, monthly and yearly goals for yourself so you have exciting things to look forward to. This can help keep your spirits up and keep you moving forward. These goals are part of the master plan you will be putting together to keep you on track.

It is important to note here no goal is too small. Some of you may be on the fast track to super stardom with a new invention that will change the face of humanity (or at least add 10 minutes to my sleep time). Others may be having a hard time getting out of bed and combing their hair. Your goals must be in alignment with a few key things: (1) where you are in your process, (2) how you're feeling currently, and (3) where you want your life to go.

If your ambitions are longer-term, such as going back to school, losing weight, starting a new relationship, or moving to a better neighborhood, it is crucial to have more immediate, sanity-saving goals that involve such things as finding some much-needed personal time, going out one night a month, listening to music, writing in a journal, getting fresh air and exercise, or spending a few minutes a day in quiet reflection.

Single mothers must take care of themselves, so include self-care goals in your plan! Make sure you eat well, sleep well, exercise, keep in touch with friends, get a manicure and pedicure, read for pleasure or even seek professional help when you need it. This will help you be the best mom you can be. When you make yourself a priority, your children will imitate that now and as they grow older. Christine understands this all too well. Participating in the program was her gift to herself. After years of putting everyone else first, she realized her self-care was non-existent and decided to do something about it. Now she practices self-care at least weekly by attending the class, and she also meditates, writes in her journal and goes for long walks by herself.

Your powerful, positive plan will get, and keep, you in the "flow state." The best way to describe the flow is that you always have more than enough of everything you need: money, space, time, love and more. It always comes to you in advance of when you need it, sometimes just in the nick of time, other times long before you actually need it. For me, just when I decide I want a new client or speaking engagement, my phone is ringing or I get an email inquiry. I meet people all the time who say, "I'm so glad we've met. The timing couldn't be more perfect." Of course it is!

Give Back

You can perpetuate your flow state by activating the Law of Giving and Receiving ... by giving. It is a universal truth that when you give, you will receive. When you're focusing on the needs of others, many times it will make your needs seem small in comparison or even inconsequential. When I think I'm having a bad day I'll see or hear from someone who makes my situation pale in comparison. As I reach out to lift them up, we both feel better. Without question, spending the last year with the single moms in the group, giving back to them, has been a priceless gift.

CHAPTER TWO

CREATE A NEW STORY

We all have a story, our own personal story of the journey that has brought us to where we are today. Chances are you can relate to "that guy," the one who cheated on you, needed a drink or drugs to make it through the day, was depressed and needed professional help (that he did or didn't get), abused you physically, emotionally, sexually or all three, spent too much time working and not enough time with you – or didn't work at all and spent all of his time on the couch, had anger issues, was a lazy slug or some combination of all of these.

Maybe it was the lack of "that guy." It could be your dad who left when you were young, or the ones that followed after that repeated the same pattern. Your lack of male role model or companionship may have left you wounded or simply feeling empty.

I get it, I really do. The reality is focusing on him is not serving you. Thinking about what he's doing or saying or what he's done or said is not taking you closer to the life you want to live, the life you are now going to start focusing on, with a genuine excitement and zest and joyfulness.

I bet you've told your story over and over and over again, sometimes to help you process through what happened, sometimes to garner sympathy, and sometimes just to throw Homer under the bus, release some anger and make yourself feel better. Did you really feel better? I don't know about you, but when I focus on the details of my failed marriage, I just get all fired up again … angry, frustrated and mad at myself for choosing him in the first (damn) place.

I have found instead that by focusing on the many blessings of the relationship, first and foremost my daughter, I can keep my positive mental attitude in check. Then I focus on the lessons learned and distinctions I made that empowered me to move on and create new and improved results in my life. Additionally, when I took responsibility for the fact that I chose him and began to dig deeper into the circumstances that caused me to do so, I began to experience something new, better and different. You can, too.

Why don't you let the last time you told your story be the last time you told your story? That's exactly what I told Laurie – I heard her story at least three times within the first week of knowing her. As a victim of spousal abuse, she left with just the clothes on her back to live in a battered women's shelter with her son. Eventually she ended up on welfare prior to starting her own business. Repeating her story was not serving her and what she was saying she wanted. By focusing on the ugly past, she was preventing herself from moving forward. It also affected her self-esteem and feelings of worthiness. Staying in that story kept her right where she was and when she took my advice, her life made a major positive shift almost immediately. Its important to note she chose to not only let go of the past, she replaced it with a new story of where she was going.

Let's change your focus to all of the cool, great and wonderful things you learned in that relationship: things you did well, things you would want to have happen again in your next relationship, distinctions you made about how to be a better partner, and choosing a better partner in the future.

The Positive Opposite List

An example of shifting your focus toward the positive is the

Positive Opposite List. This is a list of all of the things you didn't like that happened in your previous relationship(s). Then take the list and "flip it," meaning, take the not-so-positive items and write their positive opposite. Example: he cheated on you, now you want someone faithful. Whatever you focus on expands, by focusing on cheating you may very well create that again. By focusing on "I want someone faithful," you will most likely create that in your next relationship. Create your list and then take each item and make sure it is stated in the positive. Then focus on these qualities and events.

Example:

He was an alcoholic and drug addict.	becomes	He lives a healthy lifestyle.
He was abusive to me and our children.	becomes	He treats everyone with kindness and respect.
He couldn't keep a job.	becomes	He is very ambitious and reliable.

Take at least an hour to gain complete clarity over the person you want to bring into your life. There's no better time than now, while you're completely single. If you're not single, make the list anyway. That's what I did and it was an eye-opener!

Lessons Learned List

After I had repeated the same pattern of attracting basically the same guy over and over again (different name, different phone number, different address ... same frustrating, disrespectful behavior), I decided it might be a good idea to see if I could identify the lessons I wasn't getting. If I could identify them, I might be able to "get" them, which would allow me to get something better and different in my relationships.

Here is one of my Lessons Learned List courtesy of a tumultuous relationship Vicky had a few years ago:

- Its important to not force anything – ever.

- My relationships should (must! will!) be mutually beneficial, loving, etc. – give and expect to receive, too.

- I will follow my intuition, it always serves me.

- I will notice the signs – not ignore them because I don't want to see them.

- I will keep my son out of the equation until I'm sure he's going to be around for the long haul.

- Take it s-l-o-w.

- A mutually-beneficial relationship requires me to be a whole person with another whole person, and ...

- ... it should be fun and fabulous, with lots of giggling, laughing and fantastic sex.

Through this process, she learned some really interesting things about herself and what she tended to do and allow to have happen in her relationships. Once she saw it in black and white, the "a-ha!" moments were quick and gave almost instant clarity. There was no denying she needed to raise her standards and give herself some new guidelines for future relationships and her behavior in connection with them.

There is no right or wrong way to write your list. Set aside at least twenty minutes to connect with the lessons you were meant to learn and the blessings that will result in your life because you have taken them to heart.

Put Your Lessons Learned List Here:

- _____
- _____
- _____
- _____
- _____
- _____
- _____
- _____
- _____
- _____

Based on your lessons learned, you can now journal about how you would like to behave in the future, how you would like your partner to behave and what you just won't allow to happen again. This is also known as loving yourself, which in turn sets a fantastic example for the little person or people who watch your every move.

The Truth?

As women, we tend to take the things we are told about ourselves by our husbands, boyfriends, significant others, friends and family as gospel. If they say we're wonderful, brilliant, and fantastic, then we must be. If they say we are stupid, incapable and unlovable, then we must be. If you are struggling with low self-esteem that was brought on by your past relationship(s), chances are you have been told things over and over about yourself that you _believed ... even if those things are as far from the truth as can possibly be_. In order to change a belief you have about yourself, you must challenge that belief and the legs it stands on.

The Real Truth

The truth is that you are wonderful, brilliant, beautiful and fantastic ... even if its been a (long) while since that's what you've heard about yourself. The truth is you are capable, because you demonstrate it every single day by giving love to your children, keeping the lights on and the frig full, and basically getting it all done (or most of it, anyway). The time has come for you to challenge what you have been told about yourself, and frankly what you have been repeating to yourself as the truth for what may be many years at this point.

I developed The Truth Test to help you do that very thing – challenge the beliefs that are holding you back, see them as false and change them into positive, empowering beliefs that effortlessly pull you forward.

The Truth Test

First, let's look at the definition of truth, from Dictionary.com:

> Truth /truθ/ Pronunciation Key - [trooth], –noun, plural truths / truðz, truθs/[troothz, trooths]
>
> 1. the true or actual state of a matter: She tried to find out the truth.
>
> 2. conformity with fact or reality; verify: the truth of a statement.
>
> 3. a verified or indisputable fact, proposition, principle, or the like: mathematical truths.
>
> 4. the state or character of being true.
>
> 5. actuality or actual existence.
>
> 6. an obvious or accepted fact; truism; platitude.
>
> 7. honesty; integrity; truthfulness.

Let's challenge the validity of what you've been told about yourself, by others, and by you about yourself. Bring to mind something you've been told that is hurtful, and you now believe its true because it came from someone you love. Then use the Five Truth Challenge Questions to discover the truth about you, the *real* truth. Once you've identified the real truth, include them as part of your affirmation statements.

Example #1:

Old "truth": "If you were going to achieve that goal, you would have done it already. You're not good enough to make it happen. Just give up already!"

Is that the truth? No, just because I haven't achieved this particular goal doesn't mean I'm "less than" or that with more effort I won't be able to do it.

Why is it false? Because I deserve to achieve this and every goal I set, now and in the future.

How do you feel when you think its true? I feel sad, unmotivated, depressed, unworthy and like I should stop going for it.

How do you feel when you think its false? Better. I start to feel hopeful. I also start to question the other negative things I have been told about myself.

What could my new truth be? With effort, consistent, focused action and a positive attitude, I can have, do, be and create anything and everything my heart desires. I am amazing!

Example #2:

Old "truth": "You are so unattractive and stupid. You're lucky I'm here. No-one else would put up with you and your shit."

Is that the truth? No! I probably don't look as great as I used to and as great as I could (how can I with this kind of input and feedback?), but I still am a wonderful person worthy of love and respect.

Why is it false? Because I was attractive enough to attract this jackass, so there is something there – and I'm obviously smart because I am holding down a household, job and child and doing a pretty good job!

How do you feel when you think its true? I feel horrible, frustrated, depressed, unworthy and stupid.

How do you feel when you think its false? Better. I've been hearing it for awhile, so I have to start thinking differently about myself.

What could my new truth be? I am smart, attractive and capable. I am worthy of loving myself, expecting the best and having others love me, too.

Christine's ex told her that no-one liked her, the only reason she had friends was because of him. It is unanimous in this group that Christine is one of the warmest and most wonderful women we've ever had the privilege to know. He convinced her she wasn't intelligent and didn't speak proper English. For quite awhile, she didn't talk to people and even stopped talking out loud as much. With the Real Truth Test, she finally realized this belief simply wasn't true. Her new truth is, "I'm a good, wonderful, kind, loving, caring, smart, and capable friend and mother."

NOW YOU!

Do this exercise as many times as you need to in order to excavate and eliminate the beliefs that are holding you back and identify the ones that will rock your world and move you forward.

Old "truth": _____

_____

_____

Is that the truth? _____

_____

_____

Why is it false? _____

_____

_____

How do you feel when you think its true? _____

_____

_____

How do you feel when you think its false? _____

_____

_____

What could my new truth be? _____

_____

_____

Julie found several new truths during her process. "I always did what I was told, from my childhood all the way into my partnership in a CPA firm. I picked accounting because I was told to do it by my dad. Julie never stood alone. I went from my dad's house to my marital home, and was always perfect in what I did so I wouldn't ever fail. That changed with the birth of my daughter. I realized I couldn't be perfect at everything, marriage, motherhood and business. I was out of control and finally threw everything in the air. If I can't be perfect, why bother?"

After getting divorced, Julie was able to take a look at her business partnership and realized it was the same relationship she had with her dad and her husband. She was giving away her power to everyone around her and meeting everyone's needs but her own. Once she recognized her pattern, she began to make a new choice

Enrolling in this program allowed Julie to see she could take her power back and make positive changes in her life, the life of her daughter and control her future herself. Looking around, she had no friends to rely on and wasn't sure where to look. This program gave her exactly what she needed, to see other women had the same challenges and were willing to support her. Her real truth is "I am in control, can make and own my own choices. I can make anything happen on my own."

Your Real Truth List

Now that you have discovered The Real Truth, make list your new truths – preferably using the form of the "I am." Such as, "I am loveable," "I am worthy of love, loving and being loved," or "I am the greatest!" The I AM is the most powerful statement form. It is of utmost importance to speak carefully, cautiously and intentionally when using the I AM. I hear a lot of "I am unable" (also known as "I can't."), "I am stupid," "I am a horrible person," etc. Do yourself a favor – stop it! You can – and you must - use what you say after "I am" to your advantage by using those positive, empowering descriptors that make you smile when you think about using them to describe yourself.

Write Your Real Truth List in the form of your new I AM statements here:

- _____
- _____
- _____
- _____
- _____

Based on what you've created above, you now have the basis for your new story – one you will be excited, delighted and happy to share. You've taken responsibility for your part, created some new beliefs and I'm going to bet you are starting to feel hopeful and eager to get started on your awesome future.

CHAPTER THREE
GETTING THROUGH THE TUNNEL

I refer to the time between "Oh Shit Day" and "the Day the Sun Comes Out Again" as <u>The Tunnel</u>. It's the period of time when you aren't sure if you're going to make it ... to the end of the week, the end of the month, through the day at all. It sure was dark in there, I didn't laugh very much and I sure as hell didn't think I would be able to raise a happy child or fall in love and re-marry. Nope, I thought the darkness was going to last forever.

Sunlight or Oncoming Train?

My tunnel was filled with lots of words I have failed to grow fond of: depression, despair, loneliness, sadness, frustration, fear, anxiety. I remember many weekends lying on the couch and thinking to myself that if I took another nap and got another night's rest (consisting of 10-12 hours or more), I would wake up all bright-eyed and bushy-tailed Monday morning, ready to do what I needed to do to keep my businesses going, my ass small and my bank account full.

Then Monday would come and go, then Tuesday, Wednesday and Thursday, without the turnaround I was hoping for in my attitude and internal level of motivation. When Friday would come around again, I would convince myself that this would be the weekend that would be the last weekend of its kind and then

Monday morning I would wake up all bright-eyed and bushy-tailed, ready to do what I needed to do to keep my businesses going, my ass small and my bank account full. Alas, there were many more of those weekends than I would have preferred. For sure!

One of the things that finally turned me around was my coach. While she didn't co-sign my bullshit, she gave me permission to marinate in it for a limited amount of time, followed by a minimum number of actions I needed to take to get and stay on track. The limited amounts of time she gave me were "two hours" or "the rest of today." Then I was meant to cease all of the arguing going on inside of my head and just begin to put one foot in front of the other. "Action begets action" ... "a body in motion tends to stay in motion" ... "emotion is created from motion" ... these were her words, and they circulated in my head. I used what she said to encourage me when I had no courage, motivate me when I had no motivation and get me off my ass when all I wanted to do was watch television and eat lots of ice cream. Slowly but surely, as I began to do the things that made me feel better, I began to feel addicted to feeling better and wanted to feel even better ... so I did more of the activities that made me feel better and I felt better, so I wanted to do more of the activities that made me feel better ... and so on ... and so on ...

During that same time, I was also seeing a therapist. She was terrific, and she gave me tools to use for the purpose of communication that worked not only with my ex-husband but also with my clients, customers and business team. I drank every drop she gave me. I took our work together and focused on my self-improvement as I never had before. I heard more than a dozen times, from multiple sources, "I see lots of women re-marry the 'same guy' because they didn't change what needed to be changed in order to attract someone new and the new situations they wanted to attract." Uh-oh! That set me on a path that altered the direction of my life. I knew if I didn't change, I would most likely repeat history and end up right back here, only not in my early 30s with most of my life ahead of me and lots of awesome possibilities. I made the connection between my childhood, early adulthood and why I had made some of my past choices. I learned what I needed to do to heal, forgive, make plans and get on with creating an unlimited, happy and joy-filled future.

Finally, I pulled out the books, tapes, and seminar workbooks I had held onto, that resonated with me. Obviously I had kept them for a reason, and it was perfect timing when I saw them again. I reviewed them in earnest, soaking in each principle, tool and strategy, executing as many of them as I could. Very soon, I had "cracked my code." By cracking my code I mean I discovered what actions and thought processes would get and keep me moving in the right direction. I began the daily practices I still use today, the ones that allow inner peace, even when I'm in the midst of a storm. I connected my emotions with motion, realizing that exercising not only made me feel better, it also raised my vibration and I had more energy throughout the day. I made it a point to exercise five-to-six days a week ... and still do. I combined exercise with self-care including taking supplements, eating healthy (Krispy Kreme once a month only!) and getting enough rest. I started doing meditation, visualization and affirmations with reckless abandon. I started getting regular massage, manicures, pedicures and facials. I created an inner circle dream team – people who I could count on through thick and thin. I started taking care of myself and it showed. The inner work started reflecting in my outer results.

Cracking Your Code

Those three things came together in a way that really worked for me. I used coaching, therapy and constant personal development as touchstones to refocus me. As you may know, its easy to lose focus. Once you've cracked your code and gotten some momentum, you'll begin to feel more like yourself, the best version of yourself, more and more often. You'll start to feel so good that when you feel the least little bit not good, you'll immediately want to go back to feeling amazing – and you'll know exactly how to make that happen. Are you ready?

The best way to crack your code is to try different activities to find the ones that resonate best with you. If yoga sounds fun, do yoga. If reading a certain book sounds interesting, do that. The idea is to compile a list of action items that work for you. You'll refer to this list over and over again.

Alisa talks with other people, reads spiritual literature and stays in touch with people who hold her accountable. She also works on taking care of her health by eating well and exercising, which lessens her bouts with depression. She's been diagnosed with clinical depression. Rather than taking medication, she uses alternative approaches. Participating in the program helped her to clarify additional tools to crack her code.

Its important to note that there is never an end to this process. I took a personal development seminar in 2004 and tonight I'm beginning to staff it for the first time. I know I'm a different person than I was four years ago and I will hear "new" things and hear some of the same things differently. I'm excited about the changes that will occur internally, which will allow for some exciting changes to occur externally.

Beate, is a 43-year-old single mom, entrepreneur, and most recently a self-made multimillionaire. After receiving a degree in photography and being the youngest photo editor on record for Elle Magazine in her native Germany, she immigrated to the United States in 1989. Most recently she published a book, Women Who Want It All and Get It Too! A single mom since 1995, Beate has lots of wisdom to share. Her daughter, Gina, turned sixteen this year. She believes being a single mom is a world of making sacrifices and focusing on a few very important things – starting with our children and our jobs. She says she really didn't have time for anything else. She notes that getting organized and putting your priorities in order is crucial for single mom success.

In the beginning, and for many years, she didn't spend a lot of time going out, treating herself to spa weekends or fancy restaurants. While still on a budget, her self-care consisted of things that were within her reach, such as going for a bicycle ride or taking inexpensive art classes at the local museum. "It made me feel like I was focusing on myself a little but it wasn't elaborate." Beate understood what I meant when I talked about "The Tunnel." For her, this was the period at the beginning that was about self-pity and "What was I thinking? How did I pick this person?" While she never regretted having her daughter, she noted there is definitely a period of wrangling with the decision that seemed to have backfired so badly.

Her positive attitude became apparent when she said, "You say to yourself, 'I can't change it, I'm going to roll up my sleeves and move on.'" This is about making the decision that what has happened, what is happening, isn't going to break you. You're going to survive, thrive and flourish. Period.

That's exactly what she did – she started a business with very little money and eventually sold it for several million dollars to a privately-held company owned by Bill Gates. "At the end of the day, I knew I was a good person and the joke could not be on me. I refused to accept that the decisions that I had made to get married, and have a child was going to be the end. What was the spiritual message? That I wasn't going to be the loser. I was going to be the winner – I believed there was something out there for me. I accepted that the great love affair, the great marriage, wasn't the thing for me at the time. I saw other single moms – they were so angry and so hateful. I said to myself, 'I am not going to be an overweight, angry single parent that is going to eventually end up as a spinster!'"

She defines success as arriving at a point when you know you are self-sufficient, when you know you've made it. She says, "I know I've made it - I know I can take care of myself. I'm the queen of the world now, I can do whatever I want. I can relax and allow myself to enjoy the journey." Today, Beate runs a successful consulting company, is promoting her new book, watching her daughter flourish in school and out, and enjoying a committed, happy relationship.

Her message for you, dear reader, is "You're going to make it! There are lots of sacrifices but you will make it – I promise you this will pass and your day will come!" You can listen to my interview with Beate on my website at www.corpron.com.

Now its time to focus on you. Are you ready? We're going to work on cracking your code for the remainder of this book, so let's get started!

CHAPTER FOUR

IT IS WHAT IT IS – UNTIL YOU MAKE IT SOMETHING GREAT!

Life is what you make of it. You can make the decision right here and right now to create something new and different for yourself. Chances are the last three chapters have started to inspire you to do just that. When I'm inspired, I want to identify action steps so I can get results. There are a lot more action steps ahead for you.

Putting Yourself Back on the Priority List

Its important to make sure you rank high – as in first – on your list.

Melinda recalls wanting to be a mom for as long as she could remember – and now she's been a mom for more than ten years. Being a single mom, however, wasn't exactly the plan. "I recognized very early that the father wasn't going to be the best dad, so I took the steps I felt were necessary."

Even though her greatest passion in life is being a mom, she's realized after ten years she needs to focus on herself. She wants to continue being a great mom, yet understands that what makes Melinda happy and healthy is what allows her to be the best mom she can be. Its easy to lose yourself in the world of diapers, homework, backpacks, laundry, after-school activities. "You deserve that monthly pedicure!" she says, "A happy, healthy mom raises happy, healthy children."

"So when I had the chance to dive into this program, I did because I knew I could always be better. I wasn't at rock bottom, I believed there is always room for improvement and wanted to explore the opportunities to be better with the support of a group, a system, a structure."

I hope and expect that by now you have started to feel better, empowered, and hopeful. The reality is your life hasn't changed since page one and if you are at all like me, you are wondering what has to happen and what you need to do for your reality to change.

Melinda quotes Jerry Garcia, "Talk is cheap and vision true. Just saying you're going to make yourself a priority isn't enough, its making sure your feet match your lips."

Soon you will have the opportunity to create a plan – your very own shiny new 100-Day Plan. Give yourself the gift of creating this plan. It is based on the one I use every day with high-powered executives looking to take their businesses to the next level and many times turn those same businesses around completely. It is the same plan I have used with the single moms from the original transformation program highlighted in this book. Your Plan can help you to move with intention toward the life you are envisioning, beginning right now.

Why one hundred days? It is a period of time that's not too long – a year can seem like "forever" and much too long to maintain a higher level of intensity than one is used to. A month is too short – you're just really warming up after thirty days and starting to move into momentum. I've used one hundred days as my measuring stick for years and I really love the fact that it is long enough to get things accomplished but short enough that it keeps my attention. Because we're using the structure of one hundred days, you'll always know where you are percent-to-goal based on what day you're on.

Through my own personal experience, and in working with many folks through their 100 day process, I've noticed that there are definite stages that occur. You can expect to go through each of these stages, too.

- Stage 1: Excitement ... "I'm ready!" This is the initial feeling we all get when we're starting something new. This energy is enough to carry us through the beginning, which would last anywhere from one day to a few weeks.

- Stage 2: Frustration ... "Am I crazy? There's so much to do, so little time!" Your past patterns and internal beliefs start to kick in, and your mental gremlin will start to chatter and get louder and louder. That's why creating and reinforcing your new beliefs is so important. The voice in your head that tells you that you can do it needs to be louder than the voice that says you can't.

- Stage 3: Overwhelm ... "Maybe I am unable to do it all. I want to quit." This is where the rubber hits the road. You will want to quit, no matter how positive you are, how good you feel, there will come a day when you will want to stop or just settle for what you've gotten so far. Just keep putting one foot in front of the other.

- Stage 4: Ah Ha! ... "I can do it!" As you have big and little successes, those results will give you the encouragement to keep moving.

- Stage 5: Pride ... "I did it!" All of the sudden you've reached your goals, raised your self-esteem and created a new vision of what's possible for yourself. Congratulations!

These stages are completely normal. As you continue to put one foot in front of the other, all while relying on your support system, as well as the other tools and strategies I've laid out for you, you'll be just fine. I promise.

As I mentioned, I've created a pre-start checklist for you to complete prior to starting. This will set you up for success. For me, I can get very excited and dive into something head first. Very soon it becomes apparent that there's no water in the pool – oops! Or I'm all wet and there's no towel I can use to dry off with, or there's no lifeguard on duty and I'm in over my head. Sound familiar? No problem! Use your checklist to make sure you're prepared. The old saying is true: "An ounce of prevention is worth a pound of cure." Make sure when you're doing this work you have a conversation with yourself first that includes you coming from a place of what's possible and why and how you can do it. We can argue ourselves into success or into failure, so make sure your mindset is in the right place. This will go a long way toward helping you.

Coach's Note: You may not reach your goals and you will still feel pretty great about making progress. Remember: its about progress, not perfection.

Pre-Start Checklist: Get Yourself Ready

Before you can run, you must walk ... before you walk, you must crawl and to the best of my knowledge, rolling over precedes crawling. So, along that line, let's cover the basics and get you set up for success.

Here's your pre-start checklist. Prior to your Day 1, you must have completed the following seven items for maximum results:

- I have a fabulous attitude and I'm ready for massive momentum, big changes and new opportunities! (Don't worry if you're still working on your fabulous attitude – with practice, it will come. There are tips and strategies to come on how to make that happen.)

- I have chosen my Day 1 and my Day 100.

- I have completed my 100-Day Action Plan.

- I have purchased and filled out the At-A-Glance wall calendar from day 1 to day 100 (Office Max or Office Depot) and filled it out. You'll include regular calendar months and days, then track your Day 1 through Day 100. This way you'll always know where you are in the program, and how far along you should be (percent-to-goal) each and every day.

- I have purchased a Moleskine notebook (Borders or Barnes & Noble) or another kind of journal to collect all of my thoughts, ideas, distinctions, and notes.

- I have a tool to use as my calendar, to hold my database of contacts, etc. (Outlook, an iPhone, BlackBerry, Palm Pilot, or Franklin-Covey Planner).

- I have identified my Point A by answering the Pre-Start Questions.

Now you know what to do before you start your 100 days. Next, the questions that will be like Windex on your windows. They will give you the clarity you need to get started and move forward.

Pre-Start Questions: Where are You Now? Defining Your Point A.

Before we can create your new plan, there are several steps you need to take. The first, and one very important step, is to accurately assess where you are now. I call this Point A. To get clarity on your current Point A, you will spend some time with the Pre-Start Questions.

They will allow you to take an inventory of where you are right now and where you want to go. This is your desired end-game for the 100 days, your Point B. We'll be addressing what you need to do for those things to happen. Be sure to make it a point to answer these questions. Whatever you do, don't skip this step – you'll be glad you took the time to do them!

Coach's Note: These are your "so what, now what" questions. If you look at your answers and feel less than exhilarated, that's perfectly normal and completely fine. In order to reach your goals, you simply must know where you're starting. That's what these questions offer you: a true understanding of where you are and where you want to go. Nothing more or less.

Describe your life now (home environment, hobbies, vacations, relationship status, etc.).

Describe your business or career now (numbers, income, number and type of clients, etc.)

List the accomplishments, personally and professionally, you are most proud about.

List everything you are grateful for.

Based on your current results, describe what is and has been working in your life.

Based on your current results, describe what is and has been working in your job/career.

What's not working?

What activities are you currently doing (life/job/career) that could be delegated; and who could do them.

Describe your biggest time wasters (email, phone calls, co-workers, housework, etc.).

What do you need to let go of or stop doing?

What else is not working?

Congratulations on completing your questions! How do you feel? I can't lie, these were hard questions and I commend you for taking yourself on and getting clear. Many of my clients have expressed everything from sadness to frustration to aggravation with this part of the process. Let's face it – no-one thinks it's a big fun time to hold the mirror up two inches in front of our face, under bright lights, to see all of the imperfections.

Vicky felt these were the questions that gave her a huge amount of clarity. She procrastinated in doing them, and once she did she said she felt a huge weight had been lifted. "I didn't want to do the work, I knew it wouldn't be pretty to look in there. I also knew that my coach wouldn't let me slide. So I just did it anyway. The relief I felt when the exercise was completed was a surprise. I'm glad I did it."

The great news is that you've done it, you've identified your Point A and now you can begin to move forward with more grace, ease and effortlessness. Shake off any less-than-empowering feelings and let's move on to what's next.

CHAPTER FIVE
SO WHAT, NOW WHAT?

This is the first day of the rest of your life. Now that you've determined your Point A, its time to begin to envision your new future. If you're anything like some of my clients, Point A may have made you feel (if possible) even worse. Sometimes just the act of completing the questions is monumental and then to see the stark reality can be quite a bummer.

Fear not, my lovely friend! Just like going to a financial planner, determining your Point A will help you to know exactly how far it is to Point B. If you want $1,000,000 in the bank, and you begin working with a financial professional, the first step will be to determine your assets and liabilities (a.k.a Point A). Once that's done, you can come up with the plan to get you to millionaire.

The same holds true here – now that you know where you are, getting to where you're going will be a lot easier (and quicker – its always quicker when you have a map ... or in this case, a Plan).

Press Your Mental Reset Button

If you have any negative energy around your Point A, shrug it off, sister! One of my very favorite authors, Catherine Ponder (The Dynamic Laws of Prosperity), talks about the Basic Law of Prosperity which is this: what you radiate, you attract. Just like we talked about earlier, the story you may have been telling has been definitely holding you back. Now you can identify your Point B and begin to be hopeful, focused and excited about what's to come.

Put another way, you can't run east looking for a sunset ... and you can't drive forward in reverse, looking in your rear-view mirror. So stop it – right now. Trust me, you'll get where you want to go faster when you focus on there (the future) instead of here or even back there. Now is your opportunity, just like with your Pre-Start Questions, to say "So what! Now what?" That is what I mean by pressing your mental reset button. It doesn't matter what's happened up until this point, it is what you're going to do with it. As Dr. Phil says, "You either make the right decision, or you make the decision right." You are now going to make your life right, as well as your children's futures, by giving yourself a new standard to live up to, by going for it. I know you want to – so go go!

Getting to Point B

Since you've gotten this far in the book, I know you really want it – it being a rockin' fabulous future you can be proud to say you've created. Just think what an inspiration you'll be, and I'm getting ahead of myself just a bit. Set aside some time to complete these questions. This is an exciting part, trust me -- you'll love getting connected with your imagined future!

Moving Forward Questions

I know you are committed to moving yourself, your life and your children's lives forward. In order to do so, you need another level of clarity. This is truly a moment of powerful creation for you. This is where you can define the future for yourself, and this is what you can come back to again and again when times are tough. Also, when you're clear on what you want, you'll also be clear on what you don't want. This will make sorting through opportunities and situations easier as well.

Describe what you would like your life to look like within 10 years. This is your BIG VISION. Make it colorful, feel it … taste it … smell it … love it!

Working backward from your BIG VISION, describe what you would like your life to look like within 100 days.

Describe what you would like your business/job/career to look like within 100 days.

Describe the woman you know deep down you want to be (100 days from now and beyond) – and can be. Specifically: what does she look like, wear, how does she do her hair and makeup, what does her home look and feel like. Have fun with this – describe "her" in every rich detail.

Describe the mom you know deep down you want to be (100 days from now and beyond) – and can be. Specifically: how does she spend time with her children, where does she take them, what are the magic moments she creates with them, how does she model "powerful, joyful, happy woman" for them. Have fun with this – describe "her" in every rich detail.

Based on what you described above, share your level of commitment to making these desires a reality.

What needs to be in place for you to get your life in the best place to move forward.

What needs to be in place for you to get your business/job/ career in the best place to move forward.

What do you want more of?

What do you want less of?

How specifically do you need support during your 100 days and beyond?

Congratulations! You've just put in the time to imagine your glorious future. I suggest you spend some time each morning and evening reviewing your answers, envisioning, visualizing and emotionally connecting with what's to come. It will become your reality before you know it. In an upcoming chapter, we'll explore ways for you to anchor what you've created above in your subconscious mind to help it appear faster.

Alisa shared that the act of writing things in the present tense was what she needed to connect her feelings to the desired outcome. "That was huge for me. I no longer believe I will just want things, I now believe I can actually have them. As a result of that, of creating my vision of the future, things have already been set in motion. I already have more professional clothing, I got a haircut that has style. I've had huge breakthroughs in my understanding of how manifesting works." Emotionally connecting with her vision still impacts her on a daily basis.

Six Daily Actions

I have a set list of priority items I do daily, both personally and professionally that take me toward my goals: workout, read, write, marketing, coach/speak, and family time. These are my Six Daily Actions, and I've been using and teaching this practice for many years. This list is my touchstone, it keeps me focused and on track. I review it each day and calendar time to do these items, because I know when I do, I am able to reach my goals.

Christine uses these actions: She says her affirmations first thing in the morning while she's brushing her teeth. She wakes up her sons with the statement, "This is going to be a great day and everything you need comes easily and effortlessly." She listens to her recorded affirmations. She writes her affirmations. She reads spiritual books. She takes a walk and does her visualizations. "Waking up my youngest son with a positive affirmation sets the wheels in motion for him to have a fantastic day. Practicing these items is one of my acts of self-care and has helped me to create the abundant life I'm creating and living."

Once identified, the first step is to immediately calendar those six daily action items. Suddenly your list of activities will have a much greater impact on moving your life forward. It also helps eliminate the questions around where future results are coming from, and when you are taking action you simply don't have time to worry about what's next.

List the six most important things you must accomplish daily to continuously and consistently move yourself forward. Post this sheet where you can see it every day and put each item on your schedule so each item absolutely gets done!

1. _____

2. _____

3. _____

4. _____

5. _____

6. _____

Wow – you've just done a lot of work. Way to go! Can you feel the new story taking hold and getting stronger, more vivid, closer? I can! Let's capitalize on your momentum ... turn the page!

CHAPTER SIX

MANIFESTING – A WONDERFUL ALTERNATIVE TO "MAKING" IT HAPPEN

The most popular part of the program with my initial group of single moms was the prosperity work we did. A commonly known challenge single moms face is having enough money, and that was a challenge almost every mom in the group was facing. Single moms across the board report that upon their separation, their standard of living decreased substantially.

Since the moms I was working with closely expressed concern in this area, we studied, discussed and practiced spiritual prosperity laws together. Initially we met every two weeks at my house in addition to the bi-weekly conference calls. The prosperity results came quickly for most everyone: new jobs and businesses, opportunities, money, love, friendships, living arrangements, and so much more.

I define prosperity as an abundance of everything you want in your life: peace, healthy and plenty - plenty of money, time, space, love and whatever else you desire. Its not just about money, but money is certainly included. We live in a money world, a world based on a money consciousness. So its important to have plenty of it – and in my opinion an abundance of everything else we need is just as important.

When we do have an abundance of everything we need, we are able to do much more for ourselves and others. We are able to expand into our greatness and allow and encourage others to do the same. We experience less stress and more joy. I don't know about you, but I'm all about more joy! I am certainly interested in creating the life I want in the easiest and most fun ways possible. Let's dive more into how you can activate these laws for yourself and your children. You'll want to bring your friends and family in on it, too – once you're all on the same program, the synergy magnifies, hastens and expands everyone's results.

What You Are Putting Out is Coming Back to You

I've already talked briefly about the prosperity law of radiating to attract. Let's go into that idea more deeply now. I'm also going to share some other very magical and mystical ideas here that can literally change your results almost instantly. The truth is that we live on the physical plane where the results we see are the results we tend to believe. There are two higher levels, the mental and spiritual planes, where outcomes can literally be massively altered, reversed or expanded. Using these prosperity tools will help you to accelerate those results. You may have heard as a kid, as I did, "you have to see it to believe it." The opposite of that is really true, when you believe it you'll truly see it. I'll go one step further and say when you believe it, believe you deserve it and expect it to come, then you'll see it.

Remember when you were a kid and Christmas morning was tomorrow? I surely do – and I remember how excited and full of anticipation I was. I just knew there were going to be lots of pretty presents, totally fun toys I was going to play with all the next day and maybe there would even be a pony! You know what? I was always right. I would wake up nice and early, the only time until recently that's not been a problem for me, get my mom and dad, and we would open the presents. I remember getting Barbie and lots of pretty clothes for her when I was seven ... just like it was yesterday. This is exactly how the prosperity law of radiation works – you expect cool, neat stuff and cool, neat stuff comes to you.

I'm not meaning to sound overly simplistic, yet what I know for sure is that when you get excited about life, life gets excited about you. You won't always be able to determine where all the great stuff comes from, what it is going to be or when it will come. You will certainly be delighted, though, when it shows up. There's no need to be hard on yourself if you read this and instantly say: "yeah right, get excited ... probably not going to happen." Or you might want to start feeling excited, and you're afraid if you get excited and fail you'll be right back where you started. All of your feelings are okay. Notice what you're feeling, take a deep breath, and then go back to focusing on how you want to feel and what you want.

Note: the longer it takes to come, the bigger and better and more fantastic it is going to be. I know this from experience, too.

Believe You Deserve It and Expect It

There is a crucial aspect to this, and that is you need to believe you deserve what you desire. When you want something, and you don't believe it is something you deserve, it won't come to you. No matter how much you want to have a wonderful, loving relationship, live in a great neighborhood, drive a fancy car and have more money than month, if you don't believe you deserve it, it simply won't happen.

Deservability is a huge issue I tackle with a high percentage of my coaching clients, and the moms in the group were no exception. It was especially true among those who had emerged from abusive relationships. Dreaming big wasn't necessarily a challenge. It was believing that someday they, too, would find themselves at the top of the mountain.

Expecting these great new things is another critical facet of this process. I order vitamins every month, and once the order is placed, I don't question that it is coming to me. I know that in a few days, UPS will leave the box by my front door. The same is true with anything in life you want to happen or come to you. Once you've identified it and asked for it, you expect it to come. Again, simple but true.

Melinda shared with me she was told she could accomplish anything. An ice-skater in her youth, her parents encouraged her to try anything and everything. Her dad repeatedly told her, "You're the best." While not everyone is blessed with that gift, it doesn't mean you can't shift your belief and create something new and better for yourself. She believes she deserves anything and everything she wants and is grateful to already have that belief.

Her observation is that women don't believe they deserve better, so they stay in abusive situations, or simply settle for convenience or a mediocre situation instead of going for something amazing and what they truly want. "I've easily almost fallen into that trap in a relationship with someone who had a lot of desirable qualities, yet there was something missing. I knew there was something greater out there and I just had to believe in that." She goes on, "It's a huge red flag when someone tells you, 'I'm the best you're ever gonna get,' all while they're throwing things at the wall and using intimidation to get you to stay."

Right now she's using Macy's slogan: believe in magic. "I know there are magical things happening to me and coming to me."

Get in Order, Sister!

Once you've turned on the positive radiation, there are some other great prosperity activities you can do to speed up your results.

One of my favorite spiritual laws is pretty much everyone's favorite, the Vacuum Law, which in essence says that you must get and keep things in order, divine order, and get rid of everything and everyone that no longer has a place in your life to keep the good flowing your way. You've already started that process ... now let's take it to a new level. The prosperity you want doesn't flow easily into crowded, messy spaces. Emerson talked about getting into sublime order, creating order on all levels, spiritual, physical and mental.

Kelly's ex-husband cheated on her. When she found out about the relationship, which began long-distance over the internet, she was devastated. She thought this marriage was forever and it took awhile to get herself to a place where she could envision herself having more, wanting more. A friend told her within a few days, "You've got to let him go. This is not how you deserve to be treated. When you let him go, another new and better relationship will show up for you." Sure enough, she found the courage to let him go and now she's entertaining many fine gentlemen and enjoying the world of possibilities.

Clutter blocks your "chi" or energy, so eliminate the things you don't want, don't need, don't like, or remind you of someone or something unpleasant. The latter are called 'trigger devices' and each time you see them, they trigger the negative emotion associated with the person, place or situation. That negative emotion, in turn, lowers your vibration, which slows down all the great stuff that's on its way to you (or stops it completely).

Now is the time to go through every drawer, cabinet and closet. Clean them out and get them organized. Donate or give away the extra stuff that's weighing you down and make room for some shiny new thrilling things to come to you. The act of throwing things away is truly exhilarating and I find it super fun and love the instant gratification! I do it a few times a year. I always want new clothes and shoes, so when I get tired of something, I pass it on and very soon there are new items in their place. When I don't use something for more than six months, I take a hard look to make sure I still need to hang onto it. I heard once a long time ago, and then again recently, that the things you want and get eventually get you ... and have the capability of controlling how simple or complex your life gets.

When I activate the Vacuum Law by cleaning out, cleaning up, giving away, and donating, its inevitable that I receive things I want in a very short time. The other great thing is that there is an immediate sense of accomplishment when you organize a drawer, closet, or entire room. I just love putting trash bags out by the curb or dropping off items to Goodwill or the Salvation Army. I know what I'm giving away somehow finds the person who needs it.

Julie activated the Vacuum Law by asking her brother-in-law to move out of her house. He moved in promising to contribute to the household and after several months it became apparent he was never going to fulfill that promise. The day after his departure, she cleaned out of his room and placed an ad on Craig's List. Immediately she found the perfect housemate, a woman who pays her rent faithfully, takes care of her daughter on occasion and has become her good friend.

Its also a great idea to get your finances in order. Even if the mountains of debt are currently quite scary, its important to be organized and not in denial. So balance your checkbook, get all of your statements and invoices out and organized. Have a bookkeeper and CPA on your team if you're able. Taking a good look is an extension of your Point A and will allow you to get to your Point B more quickly. We'll chat shortly about how to make some drastic positive changes in your financial world.

Finally, who is in your life is just as important as your material surroundings and your finances – if not more so. We'll talk about designing and attracting your perfect support system in the next chapter. For now, begin to think about who needs to go, who needs to stay and what spaces are left to fill.

While you're cleaning up your external world, you can be working on your internal world. Its important to watch your words, what you're saying to yourself and others about you, your situation and your future actually helps to create it … no matter what you're saying! Casual or intentional, the words you speak are going out into the ethers and delivering results right back to you. Its been said that success is 98% inner work (inner preparation) and 2% outer action. The outer action is getting yourself in order.

Coach's note: Expect to receive. Ask to receive. Then wait with baited breath and positive expectation. Know its on its way to you right now.

Speak It to See It

While you're organizing those closets, you can declare, "I am in divine order, I am in sublime order now." This will reinforce to your subconscious, the part of your brain that really rules the roost, that you want to be in order and have things in order around you, even if that's not been where your comfort level (set point) has been in the past. This is the beginning of the inner work I described above.

I've long been a fan of affirmations and I've been intentionally using them for almost twenty years. I have read lots of different way to use them: say one affirmation four hundred times a day, speak words of affirmation for fifteen minutes a day, speak affirmations five minutes for every fifteen minutes you read. They all work and work very well. The trick is to do them, every day, day in and day out, for the duration. Yes, the duration of your life! My suggestion is to set aside fifteen minutes every day and speak out loud affirmations. Just like everyone else, I already use all twenty-four hours in my day, so I've had to be strategic in order to make that happen on a consistent basis.

In my car I have my affirmations written on 3x5 cards and I say them while I'm driving. I'm in the car for about 12 minutes in the morning and afternoon. So while I'm driving, I'm saying my affirmations. I also recorded myself saying them and put them on my iPod so I could listen to them and speak them at the same time. This helps me to avoid crashing into something. I've found it's a little dangerous to drive and read at the same time. I also spend some time on the treadmill a few times a week and I find that "walking and talking" really helps to raise my vibration. The moms in the Program had lots of fun with this process, and I know you will, too.

When you're reading those affirmations, be sure to say them

with spirit, with joy, and with excitement. This isn't a rote routine, an item to check off of your to do list. Saying affirmations consistently and powerfully can literally change the course of your life and hasten your results, and they can do it quickly!

Here are some of my most often used affirmations:

- I am a child of the Universe, I am a child of fortune.

- I am a money magnet, I receive money all the time, and I have so much money!

- There is gold dust in the air for me.

- God is the source of my supply. God provides his own amazing channels of supply to me now.

- I am receiving, I am receiving now. I am receiving all of the wealth that the Universe has for me.

For a complete list of my favorite affirmations, visit the Resources section of The Successful Single Moms website at www.successfulsinglemombook.com.

Writing Them Will Hasten Results

Speaking of affirmations, another valuable action is to write them. The magical number is fifteen. Take an affirmation that resonates with you and write it. How often? You guessed it, every single day. I have a giant five-subject notebook that I use just for writing my affirmations.

The ladies in my single mom's group love this idea and find that it relieves stress and keeps them out of fear. See, its impossible to be writing that you're abundant and prosperous while thinking that you're facing lack and limitation. The brain can only focus on one at the time. Let me be the first to point out that you have to continually "course correct." Remind yourself to be radiating positively. One of the ways to do this is to write down what you want to happen.

Kelly, who left her husband about two weeks before she started in the group, told me she would sit and write affirmations for hours every day. Her situation dictated that she was a couple thousand miles away from her children and she missed them terribly. She also recognized that to create a safe and abundant home for them in Las Vegas, she would need to focus on creating that, not on the terrible circumstances of her marriage and upcoming divorce.

You can also make a daily list of what you want to happen, whether it's a daily productivity goal or a financial income goal. Make those magical little lists can work wonders in your outer results.

Tithing

True prosperity has a spiritual basis. "God is the Source of your supply." Catherine Ponder was the first to introduce me to this idea, and I in turn shared it with the single moms. Whatever your beliefs, the Law of Giving and Receiving is a truth, just like the Law of Gravity. Systematic giving opens the way to systematic receiving - giving 10% of that which we have received to persons or places where you are receiving your spiritual nourishment, inspiration and information allows you to enjoy true, permanent prosperity with wondrous results.

While I'm not a minister or even an expert, I'm sharing this practice with you because it's been one of my standard practices for almost twenty years. I haven't been without financial challenges during that time, and yet I believe I have certainly lived a blessed life in large part because of tithing.

The practice of the ancient law of prosperity, tithing, has been around since primitive man offered sacrifices to his gods, including the evolving civilizations of Egyptians, Babylonians and Arabians, Greeks, Romans and Chinese. Tithing (the word "tithe" means "tenth") was a way of life. "The ancients intuitively knew that giving, sharing and putting God first financially was the first step to permanent, enduring prosperity," says Dr. Ponder. They felt that ten was the magic number of increase.

Some of the most prominent millionaires of the twentieth century attributed their extraordinary success to the practice of tithing. In 1855, as a young man, John D. Rockefeller began tithing. His total income for that year was $95.00 from which he tithed $9.50 to his church. Between 1855 and 1934, he gave away $531 million dollars. His standard reply to critics of his generosity was 'God gave me my money.' So many of the plans for becoming wealthy and rich focus on "getting" and forget about "giving." These ideas are not based on a spiritual foundation. So what are you really doing when you are giving the gift of tithing? You are saying, "thank you" for the generous bounty that you have received. You are activating the Law of Giving and Receiving.

Tithing is the act of giving gratitude for the 100% we received by giving 10% back to our Source - that is, the people or places where we realize the presence of God or whatever higher power you believe in.

Alisa, one of the single moms, wrote out a tithe check for 10% of everything she had in all of her bank accounts, even though her personal account was overdrawn. She wrote it with a trembling hand and tears in her eyes, but intuitively she knew it was the right action for her to take in that moment. The next day, she received a phone call giving her a new business opportunity. When she asked more questions, she determined the call was as a result of a conversation that took place at the exact moment she was writing the check.

"Since I have been tithing, I have more money to spend, not less," reports one student of this class. "I put in my tithe last week and suddenly the check that I have been expecting for months came in the mail." "Since the start of this class and beginning to tithe, I am receiving unexpected checks and money." The stories go on and on. I have also heard this one repeated: "I was thriving financially and in so many ways when I was in class, but I stopped tithing after it was over and I'm back in the same 'soup' I was in before."

So what can you expect when you begin to tithe?

- Fear usually shows up. I don't have enough now. How can I possibly…?

- Memories of previous associations with the word "tithe" may surface.

- Trust will become the plank to walk when beginning this practice.

- Surprise may ensue when you notice the amount of money you have to use after giving 10% to God or your source of inspiration and information.

- Doubt may surface when the above is not the immediate experience or when unexpected expenses show up instead.

- You may be surprised at the wisdom and judgment you are using to manage the money you have been given.

- You will enjoy the ease with which you are able to meet your financial obligations.

- You will notice that your connection and your spiritual life expands and your consciousness of wealth grows.

- You will find that you want to give more than 10% to a variety of places of spiritual nourishment.

- You'll wonder how you ever managed to live without tithing.

My hope for you is that you decide to give tithing a try. To the single moms, several of whom were experiencing severe stress around money, I suggested they start with 1% or even $5 as an act of faith to test the law. The reports have been 100% positive, so go for it. I know in my heart you'll find success in this practice.

Its Not Working Yet? Hang In There ... and Try This

You may have a strong desire to break out of any limitations you are experiencing in your life, and you may do each of the activities in abundance suggested above and not get the instant results you are desiring. I've been there, believe me, and more than once! Keep at it and here's why: we each have within us a "set point," much like our household thermostats. If your internal set point is currently set on "struggle," and you've been there awhile, it will take some time to change it to a new, higher level.

There are two ways to "change your mind," in other words, install a new subconscious belief that kicks in automatically, without you having to think about it. You can have or stage a significant emotional event which installs the new belief. These situations are hard to create and do not always have the lasting desired impact. Frankly, the significant emotional events you have had in the past, which installed the beliefs you live by now, probably aren't the ones you want to continue living by now and in the future. Your other option to change your mind (beliefs) is through repetition. You design a new belief, which is based on your larger overall vision, and repeat it over and over again until it becomes the belief that drives your actions, behavior and therefore results. I reference affirmations above, and the inner work that's necessary for dramatic, positive and lasting change. This is a key component of that inner work.

I am a huge fan of the book <u>Psycho-Cybernetics</u> by the great Maxwell Maltz. He suggests creating mental movies of yourself performing at your best, and viewing those movies every day. This process can be intimidating at first, and seems contrary to what we're been taught about "making" things happen. Trust me when I say the results are faster and greater than anything you could possibly expect by doing it only yourself.

Anchoring Your New Vision

Earlier I suggested there was a way to take your new vision of yourself and anchor it permanently in your subconscious mind. Repetition is the way to do just that.

Along with using the other tools I suggested, the moms I worked with for this book recorded their visions in the form of visualizations and affirmations, which they downloaded onto their mp3 players, iPods, cassette recorders (there are still a few of those floating around) or even as a message on their voicemail. Each mom wrote down their vision and a list of positive, affirmations, in present-tense form, including things they wanted to have happen but had no idea how they were going to happen. We did a 30-day experiment and the results were amazing! They listened to their recordings three times a day for thirty days. The idea was to create new neural pathways – new paths in their brains – that translated into new subconscious beliefs. You know what? That's exactly what happened!

My observation was that even the ones that didn't believe in the process whole-heartedly, yet participated whole-heartedly, had the most incredible transformations in their outlooks and attitudes.

Laurie, one of the single moms in the group, is a great example of what can happen when this process is truly, whole-heartedly embraced. When we began our 100 days, she was employed as a manicurist at a major hotel/casino in Las Vegas. Shortly after we began, she started her own company which provides personal assistant services to people who need an extra set of hands to get it all done. She wanted to spend more quality time with her son. She was on public assistance, attending ninety 12-step meetings in ninety days and living with her parents in their apartment. Her results, while small to start, were almost instantaneous – she was given a free case for her cell phone (at the dealer's store, no less), her co-pay for some much-needed dental work was waived, she received new lenses in her glasses, went to gas pump to get gas, discovered she didn't have money and magically got $20 in free gas, a lady just paid for her groceries out of the blue, a good friend paid her car payment, yet another gave her an iPod. The list of magic and miracles she experienced seemed to grow every day, almost by the hour.

Now she proclaims, "I feel so good I could jump out of my skin! I'm so excited!" Her energy is positive, powerful and simply amazing to behold! She can infect anyone within ten feet of her with her positive attitude. I have always said that the person more committed to something, in this case her intention for magic and miracles, wins. She attributes her turnaround to the new beliefs she created and then listened to three times a day.

The final results aren't in yet, but when they are I'm going to predict Laurie's grand and tremendous success! I can just as easily predict your success when you give it a try yourself.

CHAPTER SEVEN
CREATE YOUR SUPPORT SYSTEM

It would be wonderful if we lived in a world where we could do everything ourselves, and we don't. Something as simple as getting salt on your table involves between twenty and thirty people just so you could make your eggs and vegetables taste better. The truth is, we are unable to do it all alone. Heck, we are unable to do most of it alone. We need a strong, reliable support system to hold us up, bridge the gaps and keep us sane.

Now that you have a compelling vision and the supporting affirmations to pull you forward, you need the exact right and perfect people to help you get there as soon as possible.

You may or may not have the beginnings of a great support system, your "inner circle." Vicky confessed to me that her support system was literally non-existent prior to the beginning of this program. She holds a prominent position in her community and felt the need to keep her divorce and the personal struggles she was experiencing to herself. I can certainly relate! She began to open up by the third session of the program and as she did, the other ladies embraced her with a previously unimaginable amount of support. I know I said it before, there is an unlimited amount of support available to you. It is just a matter of you being open to the support and asking for what you need. Easier said than done, I know, but incredibly worth the risk. Now as Vicky looks around, the support she created is abundant and substantial.

Support System Criteria

Before you choose just anyone, it is important to put up some filters. Michael Port, the author of <u>Book Yourself Solid</u>, talks about creating a red velvet rope, just like in Hollywood, that is there for the purposes of keeping the people out who shouldn't be in. In the past, I've attempted to lean on various people during the "downs." Unfortunately, I did not always choose the members of my intimate circle wisely and ended up even more down in some cases. My take-away from that was my criteria in the choosing process needed a serious upgrade. A true friend, by my definition, is someone who walks your path with you, sees the good, the bad and the ugly and mostly ignores the bad and ugly. They are a champion for the good they see in you and encourage you to be your best – and shine a light on your darkest hours. They speak the truth from a place of love, hold you accountable for what you say you want and bring over chocolate when you need it. One of my dearest friends is someone I can call and say, "Quick! Three minutes about why I'm fabulous because I'm just not feeling it, and I need to be feeling it right at this moment!" He is always there to tell me how great I am and send me off feeling much, much better.

Vicky shared these thoughts: "If I look at the 100 day program, and the different aspects, the group atmosphere was the most nurturing and healing of any I have ever experienced. As a single mom, as someone having financial challenges, you think you're the only one ... what created change in me was being in the group. I know now it can be different, I have achieved relationships that I didn't have 100 days ago, not just with those women but with other people as well."

Support System Candidates

Your candidates are the folks that are hanging around, and maybe you've even got some others who would be delighted to be your new BFF and help you through the bad to get to the good, and then the great. In order to separate the wheat from the chaff, you must get clear. This is super important, because as I mentioned above, the wrong choices can hold you back or even take you backwards.

Let me explain it like this: there is an exchange of energy between people. If you're a ten, and I'm an eight, most likely we will end up nine. I win, you lose. If we're both tens, synergistically together we become a twenty-five. No matter what, I'd choose twenty-five over nine any day. As you begin this process, it is critical you become ruthlessly discerning about who enters, and stays, in and around you.

Action Step: List the qualities and characteristics of your ideal support system candidates. In a perfect world, imagine exactly who you want to receive support from and give support to – during and beyond this 100 days ... describe them below.

Here is a sample list to get you started:

- Positive

- Has their own vision that they are excited about and pursuing

- Thinks you're wonderful

- Helpful

- Encouraging

- Truthful

- Loyal

- Holds you capable and accountable and doesn't co-sign your bullshit, stories and excuses

- Loves you where you are and sees you reaching your goals and living your vision

Now for your list:

- _____
- _____
- _____
- _____
- _____
- _____
- _____
- _____
- _____

My support system consists of people who think I'm wonderful, smart, capable … and the list goes on. They always take my call or call me right back, and they listen until I'm finished. Sometimes this can take awhile, 'cause I'm a talker and even get paid to talk. They think my idiosyncrasies are adorable and even tease me in a loving way. They constantly ask, "So what, now what?" because they expect big things from me. When I say harsh and unloving things to myself, they don't stand for it, correct me immediately, and give me wonderful words of encouragement. Sometimes I live on those words for days, so they are much appreciated! My intimate circle knows all of my "ugly dirties" and still loves me anyway. I'm better because I have them in my corner. If you don't have a complete circle yet, that's fine. Just one person is a great start and soon you'll be on your way to more. Let's get you some new, fantastic people you can count on.

"I have never let anyone know that I was in trouble," says Kelly. "So, to go from that to asking for help and then getting it was unbelievably hard! In the past that would have made me want to jump off a fucking building. It allowed me to see that people wanted to help. I am human and I have issues. I think people don't want to help, and here I'm told to ask, so I do. I realized immediately where there's another open door. My family is nowhere to be found, and if I didn't have the skills I have I would be homeless. My opportunity is to look at that, and do something new and different and get something new and different. I am doing that and its working. No-one is more shocked and surprised than I am."

Support System List

Once you've outlined your candidates and picked the best of the best, you'll want to make sure you can get them when you need them most. All of my peeps are in my iPhone, the next best thing to speed dial.

Action Step: List the top 12 members of your support system, and their phone numbers. These are the people you can call 24/7 who will listen, offer positive advice, withhold judgment and take affirmative action on your behalf when needed. They could be friends, family, your coach, therapist, or minister. Note: There may not be 12 – or there may be more than 12 – the secret is to be ruthlessly discriminating when creating this list. When its complete, print it out and place it on your refrigerator for quick and easy access. You can always add, change or update it as needed.

One important caveat: When you choose your inner circle, all of your choices may not be perfect, or the members may change over time. That's okay, too. Just as you were selective when putting together the list, you must continue to watch to make sure your friends are truly your friends. If someone criticizes you or fails to be supportive, watch more closely. If they continue to abuse their access to your inner world, they are not a friend and should be eliminated from your inner circle as soon as possible.

Elizabeth Fernandez, a mom I had the pleasure of meeting in the process of writing this book, has long relied on a solid network that includes her best friend, her parents, her church and other single moms. "I realized early on that no matter how strong I felt, I couldn't do this alone," she says. Even now that her kids are 16 and 14, she still receives an emotional (and hands-on) booster from her team when the going gets tough. "There are days when it's hard to feel as if I'm being the best mother," she admits. "But then my best friend or another parent reminds me to hang in there or tell me she's proud of all I've done for my kids, and the morale boost helps to keep me going."

For Dori Houston, another single mom in Honolulu, Hawaii, life wouldn't be the same without her Baby Hui group of same-aged children and fellow moms, a reasonably priced handyman, a support group called Parents Without Partners, a circle of friends, and reliable babysitters. "Even though my ex-husband lives nearby and spends two evenings a week with our daughter, I'm still her primary caregiver, activities coordinator, and chauffeur," Houston says. "Without some help, I would have a tough time maintaining a balanced life."

CHAPTER EIGHT

YOUR ATTITUDE WILL MAKE YOU

I can do it! I am awesome! I am fabulous! I am terrific! I am beautiful! I am capable! I am the best mom ever!

Is this what you say when you talk to yourself? Just like the affirmations we talked about in Chapter 6, the words you use on a consistent basis reveal your true attitude. If you are saying things after the "I am" that are disempowering to you, its time for an upgrade. I have heard "I am stupid, never have enough time, unable to it," etc. Whoa! Back up! The only things you're not able to do are the things you tell yourself you're not able to do.

Moms are expected, even under the most difficult of circumstances, to maintain a happy, positive attitude. This ultimate desired state of mind; however, can be difficult to achieve when your child is sick, there's more month than money, the long to do list keeps you from getting to work on time, or you run out of milk after you've poured the cereal. Its easy to forget about maintaining control of your attitude during times like these. You're more likely to want to say, "Why do I always have to do everything myself? Why can't this be easier? Is it going to be like this forever? I give up."

A quick reminder: the quality of your life is determined by the quality of your questions. In addition, your attitude is directly affected by the quality of the questions you consistently ask yourself.

Whether you're focusing on your child's homework, completing a work project, or just paying the bills, losing control of your attitude can divert you from achieving your objective and can damage your health. Several years ago, on a trip to Laguna Beach for rest and relaxation purposes, the stress of having automobile challenges compounded by a negative personal interaction with my ex-husband reminded me of the usual challenges people face every day. I had to work hard to avoid slipping into a negative attitude.

Repeatedly, I found myself thinking of the advice I give to my clients: "Remember, the real pros (insert "mom" here) consistently perform at their peak, not because they're always in control of their circumstances, but because they're in control of their attitude." Consistently remaining committed to maintaining a Level 10 Positive Mental Attitude is key to your success. It will also pave the way for things to go more smoothly with you. I am certain my car was fixed within three hours, at a "foreign" dealership, because I "Showed Up" with a smile on my face and as much graciousness as I could muster at 8 a.m. on a Saturday morning, with my then 4-year-old in tow.

Choose Your Attitude

Conditioning yourself to having a Level 10 Positive Mental Attitude is the best way toward maintaining it. By conditioning, I mean making it a part of who you are as a person – to become positive, wake up positive and be positive. I had an abusive childhood and endured some negative experiences in early adulthood. Fortunately for me I heard a sermon given by Dr. Arthur Caliandro at Marble Collegiate Church in New York City very shortly before my 20th birthday. The title of the sermon, which I will never forget, was "You CAN Do It!" Part of his message was about the choices we make and how they make us who we are and determine what happens to us in the future. I decided right then and there to choose happy and to do whatever was necessary to be happy. For me, that meant going for long walks up and down Park Avenue, admiring the beautiful buildings and listening to Billy Joel's Greatest Hits on my Walkman. This beat the heck out of sitting in my one room studio apartment and lamenting my current state. When I got home, I was sweaty and in a really great mood. I did this every evening after work. Pretty soon, I started to wake up happy. The conditioning had begun.

The questions we ask ourselves are a large percentage of the attitude equation. 'What's great about this?' feels much better than 'Why does this always happen to me?' or 'How can he/she/ they do this to me?' A positive question most likely isn't your first reaction, that's ok. Back to conditioning – the first step in this part of the process is to notice the questions you're asking yourself, and then ask a question about the question, "Is this the best question I can be asking?" Tony Robbins' Unlimited Power seminar was one of my first experiences with personal growth. In his book, Awaken the Giant Within, he suggests the use of Morning Power Questions. Here are a few of mine, which I put on a 4x6 card taped to the wall in my shower, so I could read them first thing in the morning:

- What am I excited about?

- What am I grateful for?

- Who do I love and who loves me?

- What am I looking forward to?

- What are my top 3 goals and what will I do today to reach them?

Actions are what reinforce what you say you want to your sub-conscious mind. It is so incredibly important to identify the actions you will commit to take, and these actions will begin to override your beliefs and the results of the past. My actions include: working out for 20-30 minutes six days a week, writing and speaking affirmations, doing visualization and meditation, spending quality time with my family, friends, reading or nothing (so I can recharge, of course).

Christine is a great example of someone who has chosen her attitude, and her results have followed suit. When we first started, she was in a miserable job, and there was no chance for advancement within the company. She had taken a pay cut to work at home and wasn't making enough money. She says, "I was miserable!" She had no idea what she wanted, and had no idea how to get there if she did know what she wanted. She dove into the Program and intentionally upgraded her attitude through her questions and actions. Almost immediately she started her own business and after just six months the revenue is starting to really flow.

Prior to the Program, she had been reading and learning everything she could about The Secret Movie and Law of Attraction and for her it just wasn't clicking. She understood it but didn't know how to apply it to her life. She says, "I had heard of coaching, and everyone I knew who had gotten anywhere in their life or business had or has a coach. I knew I had to get a coach, but had no way of getting a coach because I didn't have any money. So what I focused on, what I kept focusing on was I needed a coach. I knew I wouldn't be able to find my way, get where I wanted to go unless I got a coach."

She got an email about the Program from Alisa, who posted about the Program a few different places online. She applied for the Program immediately and her questionnaire was as passionate and full of commitment as she could make it. "The Universe sent this to me and I must be in the program!" she declares. You can clearly see she has the makings of great success in large part because of her attitude.

Attitude development and control involves the practice and application of three peak performance skills:

Effective Self-Coaching

When Michael Jordan quit basketball to fulfill his father's wish that he play baseball, reporters asked him: "How can you quit basketball after being voted the most valuable player? What if you fail at baseball?"

Michael Jordan, a master at playing in "The Zone," where nothing distracts him from giving his best performance, said: "I'm strong enough as a person to face failure and move on. If I fail I won't feel bad. I can accept failure. What I will not accept from myself is not trying."

In that one statement Michael Jordan tells us that -- regardless of the odds and regardless of the outcome -- he will be there for himself, on his side all the way through the game. Effective Self-Coaching means that we offer ourselves safety rather than threats, criticism and worry. Like Michael Jordan we need to be strong enough as a person to be an effective coach in our lives — staying focused on core principles, recovering from setbacks, and making ourselves feel safe enough to take the risks that make us champions in our field.

Effective Self-Coaching includes supporting and motivating yourself on a consistent basis. Be sure to keep quotes and pictures that inspire you all around you. As a peak parenting performer, having triggers around you to keep your attitude on track can make a huge difference ... and keep the trajectory of your life and your children's lives moving in the right direction.

Shifting to a Leadership-of-Self Perspective

The gremlins inside our heads complain and whine, distracting us from doing our personal best. Identify the specific words and feelings of these gremlins and be ready with alternatives that shift your attention to effective, goal-oriented actions. Use your usual or "default" reactions to stress and setbacks to wake-up the leadership role and perspective in you. From this perspective and role, of mom, friend, daughter, business owner, coach or classroom helper, we can take charge of our attitude and our life.

Ellen, one of my executive coaching clients, single mom, and the managing partner of a technology services firm in northern California, used this technique to double her income in three months and begin focusing on what was really personally important to her. After her divorce, she found herself overwhelmed with responsibilities and activities – all needing to be addressed and completed by her. She says: "I used to work with my nose to the grindstone, faxing at 3 AM, totally out of touch with my commitments to my health and my children. Now, I'm doing the work that relates to the bottom line and I'm done before 7 p.m. I'm working from a project manager's perspective where I see the big picture, focus on getting results, and maintain my commitment to my personal life."

Personal leadership means taking responsibility for your life and how you want it to flow, to look, to be. Remember, "Its your life. Take control and make it the way you want it to be!"

Choosing to Show Up

When we're in charge of our attitude, we don't use the victim's inner dialogue: "I have to show up but I don't want to." Instead we speak about "choosing to and wanting to show up to do our best." Choice is a function that involves considering the risks, consequences, and one's commitments before deciding how to act. Choice is an act that ends ambivalence and procrastination and calls for a focused effort to achieve an objective. It automatically puts you in a leadership-of-self role and perspective.

Keep in mind the speed of the leader is the speed of the pack. Your attitude, as the leader, determines the attitude of anyone and everyone around you – including your children! I love the answering machine message of one of my favorite people, her message ends: "Is your attitude worth catching? If so, leave me a message. If not, call me back when it is!" I recently heard something interesting – an army of sheep led by a lion will defeat an army of lions led by a sheep every time. Who you are being, how you Choose to Show Up, determines your success, your stress level, who you have and don't have in your life ... and ultimately your bottom line.

When your child gets sick (again), when there's another challenge with your ex-husband, friend or brother-in-law, or when loss or illness disrupts you personally, you're still expected to carry on. To consistently deliver -- regardless of the setting and circumstances — you'll need something more powerful than the old "grin and bear it" technique. You'll need to support yourself with the safety of Effective Self-Coaching, rapidly shift to a Leadership-of-Self Role and perspective, and Choose to Show Up to demonstrate that you truly are a force to reckon with and a fantastic mom to boot! When you use these skills you'll be in control of your attitude. The results, I am positive, will delight you.

Repeat after me: "I can do it!"

Your Power Words

I do a lot of reading in the personal development realm, and I see a lot of recurring themes among the successful, wealthy, and happy crowd. One of the most interesting things I've discovered is that the words they use to describe themselves to themselves are positive, powerful and compelling, driving them to take action because that's what they expect of themselves.

It is great to have three words you use to describe yourself that increase your joy. Remember, I'm all about joy. It is very important to use positive, powerful words when describing yourself – to identify them, memorize them, and use them. Again, its very easy to fall into the trap of being self-critical. As my basketball coach father used to say, "The best defense is a good offense." The application here is that since you know the defense (self-criticism) is coming, prepare a great offense (your power words) so you can stay on track.

Give yourself three "power" words, the three **incredibly posi-tive** words you will now use when describing yourself, words you will now use *daily* after the words: "I am."

1. _____

2. _____

3. _____

The first night of the Successful Single Moms Transformation Program, the moms had an interesting time with this exercise. They seemed to have a little bit of a hard time finding even three positive words to say about themselves. They asked questions in an effort to stall, "Is this just a word about me? Or is it about my whole situation?" My suggestion is to dig deep and put down the words that take your breath away right now – the words that when they come true will bring tears to your eyes. Dare to see yourself as bigger and better and more fantastic than you have ever dared before. Do it anyway – no-one needs to see them but you. Most importantly, you need to see them.

Affirmations for Success

Using affirmations allows your subconscious mind to help you speed up your results. What? I've said that already? Yes, I know! Affirmations and affirmative statements are all over this book – and I'm saying it again because that's how important it is!

Spend at least thirty minutes each day speaking, writing and meditating on the following statements. Pick one statement and repeat it as many times as you can throughout the day and write it at least 15 times. Doing these statements while power-walking or running anchors them in your subconscious mind for increased and accelerated results.

- I create my life. I create the exact level of my success.

- I play full-out with the intention to win.

- I admire and emulate successful and balanced people.

- I deserve success, love, happiness and the very best of everything!

- I believe success is important, success allows me to have liberty, and I enjoy my success.

- I become rich and successful doing what I love.

- I deserve to be successful because I add value to others and the world.

- I am truly grateful for my success.

- Opportunities to increase my success consistently come my way.

- My capacity for greater success continues to expand day-by-day.

- I expect success.

- I attract success to me like a magnet. Success comes to me as if by magic.

- I am an irresistible magnet for unlimited money, clients, goods, services and opportunities every single day!

Your True Qualities & Characteristics List

List the truth about you – as you see it now and as you want to see it in the future. These are your qualities and characteristics – the words that describe the best, most amazing version of yourself.

Here are some of mine:

- awesome mom

- lovely
- kind
- honest
- giving
- loyal
- focused
- on time
- fiscally responsible
- business genius

This is another way to do the I AM exercise from a few chapters ago. No, its not a typo, its intentional on my part that I help you focus on the great parts of yourself. So if you skipped over it the first time, here's a slightly different way to look at it and *do it*.

Some of these you will grow into over time. That's ok – list them now as if they are present-day truth. You identified in your Point A questions the woman you want to be in, the mom you want to be. Chances are you identified some of these qualities and characteristics.

You become what you think about, what you focus on. You have a golden opportunity here to create your future in advance – and then, if you really want to, you can step into that future today.

Keeping Yourself Happy: Your Happiness Action List

This is your "to do regularly" list – the things that make you smile, giggle or even feel giddy. Here are a few from my list: eat chocolate at any temperature, workout, spend quality time with my daughter, go for a drive to some fantastic music (note: must observe speed limits), read a great book, watch an inspiring movie, chat with a girlfriend, take a hot bath, go to a bookstore, read a trashy magazine and drink a chai latté. You'll refer to this list at the end of a hard day, at the beginning of a Saturday when your kids are with their dad or just whenever you need to feel better *now*. You can even keep a copy of this list on the refrigerator right next to your inner circle list. Call someone for a boost of positive energy or eat a piece of chocolate? You decide.

By creating this list, you will just be a few seconds away from reminding yourself what makes you feel good – and some of your items will be in the cheap-to-free category, you won't have any reason to not do one or several of them until you feel much better.

My wonderful new husband takes a break at the office and "shoots aliens" when he's had a long stretch of working or is stressed about a particular situation. Rather than trying to "muddle through" or turn his frustration outward, he got in solution mode and thought about how good he feels after a few minutes on his Xbox. Turns out it's a great stress reliever. I can hear the out-loud, belly laughs all the way into my office. When he comes out of the conference room after just 10-15 minutes of game play, he's a new man.

Now for your list:

- _____
- _____
- _____
- _____
- _____
- _____
- _____

By now, you've gotten some tools for your toolbox to help you achieve your vision and goals. What's next is what you've been waiting for: creating your plan. I'm ready when you are!

CHAPTER NINE

CREATING AND IMPLEMENTING YOUR FIRST 100-DAY PLAN

We've covered a lot of ground and laid a lot of groundwork. You've done a lot of work already, and yet another pat on the back and moment of celebration is in order. Now is the time to create the plan to get all the things you've identified you want! I chose the format of 100 days because its long enough that it allows someone to make significant impact on their life, yet it is not too long. Setting annual goals is fine, and its easy to let yourself off the hook and have a lower sense of urgency when you have a much longer time-frame to complete your commitments. A 100 day time span requires a high sense of urgency. You must be committed because the days go by very quickly!

The moms from the Program used a version of the 100 Day Plan I use with executives in my coaching practice. I told them at the first meeting that the time would fly by and soon our fourteen weeks together would be over. At our final session, they marveled at several things, one of which was how incredibly quickly the time had passed. Another was the remarkable changes and transformations that took place within the group.

The initial meeting was to discuss the Program, how it worked and what the participants could expect to happen as it progressed. The ladies, for the most part, didn't know each other. We were coming together to discuss intimate details of our lives up to that point, to share our struggles and to put together an action plan to move forward. You now have the same opportunity

– to design how you would like the next 100 days (and beyond) to go for you. Are you ready? Let's begin!

To get started on your Plan, review the definitions, below:

100-Day Action Plan Definitions

Dates:

This is Day 1 through Day 100.

100-Day Vision:

This is your "what." What do you want to accomplish, bring to fruition, achieve over the next 100 days.

100-Day Purpose:

This is your "why." What would accomplishing your goals and objectives give you, provide for you, help you to achieve down the road?

Top 3 Goals:

The three most important things you wish to accomplish during this Program. Make them SMART: Specific, Measurable, Attainable, (at least a little) Risky, and Time-sensitive. The deadline for these goals is, of course, your 100th Day. These could include: spending more time (quantified) with your children, losing/gaining weight, starting or completing a project, a business-growth goal, etc.

Empowering Descriptors:

This is the fun part – give yourself a reputation to live up to! Use phrases that turn you on and rev you up! My empowering descriptors include: Mother of the Year! Queen of Manifestation! Best Mom Ever! Super Balancing Genius!

Three areas of focus:

These are the three areas of your life you want to focus on during the Program. They could include: raising your self-esteem, your health, getting organized, growing your client base, or focusing on family time or your faith.

Resources:

These are the people and things you can rely on – really rely on – during this 100 days and beyond. Refer to Chapter 7, Creating Your Support System.

Next Steps:

This is your "data dump." Get out of your head and on paper every single thing that needs to get done, regardless of whether or not it (a) has anything to do with your goals and (b) has to be done by you (or right now you think it does). These items could include cleaning out your car, doing follow-up calls, buying cat food or sending a card to your mom. If you're carrying it around in your head, it's adding to your stress level and making you less effective. Take your list and put the items in order of importance. Your items will fall into one of four categories: Do, Delegate, Delay or Dump. Take a few moments to categorize and assign the tasks to delegate to the proper individual. (Coach's Note: This list is not limited to the space provided.) Once completed, put in order of importance and schedule as many items as possible on your calendar. This will give your brain a rest, because once its on your calendar you can forget about it until it pops up on your schedule.

Next, its time to do your 100-Day Action Plan. I've included one in this book, and you can also download one at http://thesuccessfulsinglemom.blogspot.com. Complete your Action Plan prior to your Day 1, so that you're ready for your actual Day 1 and you start the day knowing your action steps!

The Successful Single Mom
100-Day Action Plan

Dates: _____

100-Day Vision:_____

_____

_____

_____

_____

_____

_____

_____

100-Day Purpose: _____

_____

_____

_____

_____

_____

_____

_____

Top 3 Goals

1. _____

2. _____

3. _____

Describe why you MUST achieve these goals: _____

_____

_____

_____

_____

Empowering Descriptors

- _____
- _____
- _____
- _____
- _____

Three areas of focus:

1. _____

2. _____

3. _____

Resources:

1. _____
2. _____
3. _____
4. _____
5. _____

Next Steps:

1. _____
2. _____
3. _____
4. _____
5. _____
6. _____
7. _____
8. _____
9. _____
10. _____
11. _____
12. _____
13. _____

14._____

15._____

16._____

17._____

18._____

19._____

20._____

21._____

22._____

23._____

24._____

25._____

Once you've gotten it completed, give a copy to the person or people you've designated to assist and hold you accountable during this time. These could include your coach, members of your inner circle or even your therapist. If you're interested in creating your own single mom's transformation group, we'll be covering the how-to's in Chapter 11. Make sure whoever you show your plan to is 100% for you, so the support you receive is the support you need.

Enjoying the Journey

This entire process, including your initial 100 days and the many that will follow, is meant to be savored. This is not at all about perfection, this is about you reveling in the fact you have taken yourself and your circumstances on and are making positive changes for your future. The lasting impact this will have on your life and the lives of your children are immeasurable and yet will be tangible and remarkable. Much like in life, you may experience days that are fantastic, where you are so excited you can hardly stand yourself. Other days, you will want to just stay in bed. Know that where you are and what you are feeling is just fine.

I read in a magazine a few years ago that when you have what seems like an overwhelming project or list of things to do, you can set the timer for ten, fifteen or twenty minutes and then work on what needs to be done fast and furious until the timer goes off. At that point, you give yourself permission to stop if you haven't really "gotten into it." I think I've used that technique more than a thousand times to get myself to workout, clean the kitchen, fold laundry, get some work done or just do some general housekeeping. It works like a charm for me, and the moms found it helpful, too. The next time you're feeling under-motivated, give it a try.

CHAPTER TEN
DAY 101 AND BEYOND

When your initial 100 days is complete, you may once again being feeling a mix of emotions: relief, happiness, joy, frustration ... or a mix of those and many others. This is completely normal! When my corporate coaching clients complete a 100 day program, we do a review and observation which includes discovering the answers to these questions:

- Describe what went right.

- Describe your results.

- Did you reach or exceed your goals? Why or why not?

- What did you learn about yourself?

- What else did you learn?

- What was the greatest benefit of the program to you?

- What results do you expect in the next 30-60 days as a result of the program?

- What are the opportunities that have become available to you because of your activity over the past 100 days?

- What results do you expect long-term because of your activity over the past 100 days?

- What did you not do, or do enough, that you could do more of in the future to increase your level of success?

- What didn't work about the program?

- If applicable, what could your coach/group do better or differently?

- Would you like to participate in another 100 day program? Starting when?

- Who do you know that would benefit from the program as you have benefited from the program?

You will get some unexpected clarity from answering these questions, just as when you answered the pre-start questions. I do this exercise myself after completing each 100 days and I always discover a few things that hadn't occurred to me during the process.

If you're anything like the original group of moms, you'll want to continue immediately. Our 100th day celebration, which I hosted at my house, was such a delightful event. My house was at least six inches off the foundation – the energy was so positive and powerful! While our pre-start gathering was a great evening, by the 100th day, everyone knew each other really well. Each person had walked this part of their journey with the support, caring and love of the other participants.

One of the most powerful aspects of the Program is the internal transformation that translates into others responding to you in a more positive and happy way. Your attitude becomes more positive, in large part because you've now proven to yourself what you're capable of when you commit and follow through with something that initially seemed daunting and impossible. You argue for the possibilities, rather than any perceived limitations. You find the general public more friendly – I certainly do! There are random acts of kindness, unexpected gifts, cash and services that come your way. You find yourself saying "yes" to things that before you said "no!" to.

The External Part of the Transformation

My inspiration for this book began while watching the Oprah show. The program that day featured makeovers of "schlump-adinks," which I believe is defined as a woman who dresses in sweats, hasn't colored (or even combed) her hair in quite some time ... is basically a woman who has let herself go. It is so simple and easy to put yourself last on the list.

Does this sound familiar? "I'm just running to the grocery store, post office, to drop off the kids at school. It doesn't really matter I'm not put together, right? Its not like I'm going to run into anyone and ... I'll be back in just a few minutes."

The truth is, it does matter! It doesn't necessarily matter because of what other people think, it matters because of what you think. The truth is, we are judged by how we present ourselves. It would be a shame if someone dismissed you or discounted your credibility because of how you showed up. I know I feel a thousand times better when I take a few minutes to put on a cute pair of shoes and some lip gloss. If my hair is in a scrunchie, I'll pull it out, do a quick braid, a fun ponytail or at least make a French twist. I have filled my closet with classic basics so dressing in a minute is a breeze. The truth is, we all feel great when we look great. Be sure that you give attention to how you're presenting yourself to the world. You're taking yourself seriously and I want the world to take you just as seriously.

If you're not sure where to start, no problem! If hair and make-up are your concern, turn yourself over to the experts. Visit any department store make-up counter and you can get a free make-over with the option to purchase some, all or none of the products they use to give you your new look. For my recent nuptials, I went to the Bobbie Brown counter at Nordstroms and had a really fun hour playing around with color.

Clothing and fashion, at least for me, had never come easy. I am a faithful *What Not to Wear* (on TLC) viewer and rule-follower (thanks Stacy, Clinton, Nick & Carmindy). Tim Gunn's **Guide to Style** (Bravo) is a new personal favorite. There is an endless list of books and online resources you can visit to get your start.

The Transformations

When Vicky started the Program, she had three goals: 1. Create a business that would allow her to provide for herself and her son; 2. Get organized financially and decide next steps (reorganize debt, engage in credit counseling, file bankruptcy or make a settlement offer); and 3. Exercise daily for 30 minutes.

She says, "I consider my participation in the Program a success because it opened up things to me that were necessary. It helped make the opportunity to look at what was working, not working, and to shine the light on that dark in a safe place with like-minded people was very helpful, very useful. It was truly life changing."

Present day: her business has been established, for the first time ever in her life she completely looked at her finances, got into them and got herself, in her words, "covered in the mud of them," and began to exercise and reevaluate her relationship with exercise – not what it had meant in her life, but what it could mean in the future in terms of how she wanted to live her life.

With Christine, she didn't know what to expect that first night at our initial meeting. She was excited she could relate to the coach (me), the other ladies and the Program.

That enthusiasm was dampened a bit as she began answering the questions. She felt overwhelmed, like she had taken on more than she could chew, and she got really nervous. "I did homework the first week. Did everything I was supposed to do the first week. The second week, I didn't do hardly anything, felt horrible, bad, guilty. After the first call, I felt better because I wasn't the only one having a hard time getting started." After every call and with the addition of prosperity class, she felt better and better.

She started her new business within a few weeks of the class. At first her old boss wanted to sue her, and she was pretty sure she wasn't going to make it. After a brief conversation with me, she started writing her affirmations for a day and a half. "I just wanted it to go away." Christine said. That is exactly what happened.

As of today, she has built a website and gotten fifteen customers and the business keeps growing. By the end of the year, she will be in the black, making more than enough money to pay her bills with an abundance of money. She just knows that things are going to get even better as time goes on. You know what? I know it, too.

For more of the mom's transformations, visit them at http://thesuccessfulsinglemom.blogspot.com.

CHAPTER ELEVEN

CREATE YOUR OWN SUCCESSFUL SINGLE MOM TRANSFORMATION GROUP

There are a couple of ways to share the Program with others. You can pass on this book to other single moms you know, with a word (or note) of encouragement, a high five, and wishes of good luck. That's great and we'll both appreciate it. (Smile.)

Creating Your Own Group

Another option is to put together a group of your own. Let me say at the outset that you will be delighted that you have! Here are my suggestions for putting together your group, and the tried-and-true format that works.

To spread the word that you're creating a group, start by emailing everyone you know. As it turns out, there are single moms everywhere who want to connect with others in the same situation and become supportive to one another. Everyone is a single mom, knows a single mom, was raised by a single mom or was once a single mom. You will find an abundance of prospective group members if you tell enough people what you're looking to find. You can also send a press release to announce the Program and get interest that way (that's how one of the women ended up in the group, her employer is a media company and she read the release and gave me a call). I posted a notice on my blog. I told everyone I could find about the Program and the group really could have been twice as big.

Vicky expressed that she didn't know there were so many other women who were like her and dealing with the same issues. "What I found most important about the entire class was the solidarity that it brought. Having Honorée as the leader created a place where we could only be positive, only look forward at the positive, take stock of what we were grateful for, get out of our ruts, and use the tools that were given. Those tools were priceless."

Finding the Perfect Members

As with choosing a job, a life partner or a housekeeper, selection is key. When you put together the right group, the results will be magical and astounding. I personally didn't know a lot of other single moms when I set out to write this book, now its amazing to me the number of single moms there are running around. I created a survey for interested moms to fill out through www.surveymonkey.com. I did this for a couple of reasons: I was giving of my time, resources and information, and what I wanted was a group of women that would dive in, head first, and be committed to the process ... the entire process.

Here are the questions I used:

- What is your relationship status?

- How long have you been a single mom?

- How many children do you have?

- Tell me what you want most for your child/ren.

- Tell me what you want most for yourself.

- What is your biggest challenge as a single mom?

- Describe your self-esteem in 3-5 sentences.

- If you have enough support, what would you decide to do?

- Describe your top 3 most important goals.

- Tell me why you would be the perfect addition to a Successful Single Mom Transformation Program Group – and share your level of commitment to doing the work and completing the Program.

You can use my questions, create your own, or use a combination of both. After you have more than enough ladies interested, you interview them to find out more about them. I was interested to know how long they'd been a single mom, what their current challenges consisted of, and whether they could give to the other members of the group. (You don't just want takers, people who come to the group and get what they can. They need to come from a place of giving, what they get will be their bonus.) I also wanted women with a positive attitude, or at least the makings of a positive attitude. Coaching is a volunteer, opt-in process. Its imperative to have participants that are open to hearing the truth, shifting for the positive, and being a source of good energy and inspiration for the other members of the group.

The ideal size for the group is six to ten women, including the facilitator or leader of the group. Having an "even number" of women allowed each woman to "buddy up" with someone. During the Program, when a mom didn't show up for a call or complete her homework, I relied on her buddy to reach out and find out what was up. It's the buddy's job to make sure her partner in the Program is okay, provide needed support and encouragement, and be a voice for the person who perhaps is without her voice. She can report to the group that her buddy needs support and that in and of itself is extremely valuable. Its not that you can't do that, it just that you want as many connections between the women to occur as possible – and you probably won't have time to keep track of everyone yourself. You are a single mom yourself, after all.

Be sure to insist on complete confidentiality. This will create safe space for each mom to share.

Helpful Guidelines for Making It Work

You will have the best and most productive meetings if they are in person. I hosted the gatherings in my home and allowed the women to bring their children. The children played with my daughter in her room, or watched a movie, or played tag outside while we got together. Since we've continued, my daughter starts getting ready days in advance of our Tuesday night meetings. You can move them around to different places, or have them in one place for consistency.

Our meetings start at 6 p.m. and go until around 7:15 p.m. This seems to be the magical time that everyone could attend – they were off work, they could get to the meetings on time, and have enough time to get home and put the kids to bed before it was too late.

Since it is the dinner hour, you can create a snack list or do potluck. After a few weeks, many of the moms started arriving around five o'clock to feed their kids, and have some time to socialize.

The Program's Meeting Format

To keep the meetings productive, moving along at a nice speed and ending on time, I used the guidelines from Alisa's former mastermind group. We went around the group for each of the following:

- To start, each mom shared her accomplishments for the prior week. These are the "deliverables" – what each lady said she was committed to accomplish before this meeting.

- Then we moved on to the "wins" … different from accomplishments in that it could have been spending time with their kids, getting a new client or just getting out of bed before noon seven days in a row.

- Next were their goals for the upcoming week. These are the deliverables for the next meeting, and they are meant to be specific. We didn't stop at "more money" or "additional exercise," everything is quantified so accountability can be at it's peak. If necessary, we helped each mom identify action steps.

• Finally, each mom had an opportunity to ask for what they needed. Sometimes it was help in distributing a resume, childcare so they could get some work done or take a nap, or just someone to listen.

As I mentioned, we finished the original 100 day Program and the ladies were unanimous they wanted to continue. We still meet every Tuesday night in my home and there are no signs of stopping.

Now you can become a facilitator or join a Single Mom Transformation Program class near you. Visit http://thesuccessfulsinglemom.blogspot.com/p/find-class.html

CONCLUSION

YOU ARE A SUCCESSFUL SINGLE MOM

You have my deepest gratitude for reading this book – thank you. I want to commend you for taking the time to read this book – in doing so, you have proven your commitment to yourself and your children. What comes next is going to be amazing for you. There will probably be a few moments of yucky thrown in for good measure, just to make sure you're paying attention and really committed to the amazing-ness you say you want.

What's next is truly up to you – and the possibilities are endless! From my heart to yours, I want you to hold out what for what you really want. Never settle, never accept second best – go for what you want every single day.

You can do it, so do it. The best is yet to come.
To Your Success, Joy & Happiness,

Honorée

Not Without You

To my "inner circle." You know who you are. I remain in awe of you. Thank you for your love and support.

To the single moms – Our journey together has been more than I ever could have hoped for - I have learned so much from you and honor you. Thank you.

To Lexi - Thank you for being such a wonderful daughter! You inspire me to be the best mom I can be. I love you with all of my heart.

To my wonderful husband – You were the person I was waiting for all this time. Thank you for being such an incredible blessing. Every great thing in my life, especially this book, wouldn't exist without you. I love you.

To Dino Marino – You brought this book to life in pictures and design. Your ability to capture the essence of what I am attempting to convey is exceptional. I am forever amazed and grateful.

HONORÉE

AUTHOR. Honorée is the author of the books *Tall Order!*, *The Successful Single Mom Cooks! Cookbook*, and *The Successful Single Mom Gets Rich!* She created The Single Mom 100-Day Transformation Program, The STMA™ 100-Day Action Plan Coaching Program, and The Tall Order! Success System and The Referral-Only Business System self-study courses.

SUCCESSFUL SINGLE MOM. Honorée is the proud mom of Lexi, a precocious 9 year old third-grader who teaches her new things about success every day. She does her very best to live what she teaches ... and she teaches it so she remembers to live it.

BLISSED OUT NEWLYWED. Using the tools in this book prepared her to attract and marry her fantastic new husband, Byron Corder.

ENTHUSIASTIC MENTOR. She coaches single moms to live their ultimate lives through her ground-breaking Single Mom Transformation Program. She teaches an Effortless Living class in her home for single moms, moms and women interested in living a life of abundance and happiness.

SINGLE MOM BLOG. Her blog reaches thousands of single moms each week, providing tips, tools, strategies, ideas and recipes for making the most of yourself, your mommy-ness, and your life. Visit and subscribe at: www.successfulsinglemombook.com

SINGLE MOM TRANSFORMATION PROGRAM. Learn more about this program, based on *The Successful Single Mom* book, at http://thesuccessfulsinglemom.blogspot.com/p/find-class.html

Honorée Enterprises, Inc.
www.honoreecorder.com
www.thesuccessfulsinglemom.blogspot.com
www.twitter.com/singlemombooks
Honoree@honoreecorder.com

CPSIA information can be obtained
at www.ICGtesting.com
Printed in the USA
BVOW03s1914081216
470232BV00010B/398/P